W9-CGT-932

The
Standard Question Book
and
Home Study Outlines

The Frontier Press Company

Buffalo, N. Y.

1919

PREFACE

The days of the cave man have passed. Physical strength alone no longer gives prowess to the individual. What the twentieth century demands is the trained intellect. The man who *knows* is the man of the hour.

A very large percentage of all fundamental knowledge is and must be gained through books. They are the storehouses of the world's wisdom from which we all must draw; but of the making of books there is no end. More than ten thousand new ones make their appearance each year. As this process continues from year to year, the world's wisdom becomes more and more scattered. In every book that aims to be instructive there are some things of value while in many there is much that is irrelevant.

It has well been said that, if all the book knowledge of the day could be sifted through a fine screen and only the best things preserved, the process would be highly beneficial to all seekers of wisdom. It was this thought that prompted the building of The Standard Dictionary of Facts. This practical and very instructive work has now been on the market for several years. Its contents have been greatly improved and its sale has greatly increased with the passing of each year. The American people have already invested over three million dollars in the purchase of this single-volume book and those intelligent purchasers are enthusiastically recommending it to their friends.

When The Standard Dictionary of Facts was first issued it was accompanied by a small book of questions designed to call attention to the great mass of information within the one volume. The questions were divided into chapters corresponding to the divisions of the complete book. There was no attempt at further classification. In each chapter the questions were miscellaneous. The little question book went into thousands of homes; it was enthusiastically received. The publishers were surprised by the demand for it made by their sales organization.

Gradually there developed in the minds of the publishers the idea that additional material with careful classification would render such a book of questions more useful and with this thought in view the present question book has been prepared.

The subject matter is divided into fourteen distinct groups embracing approximately seven thousand questions. One particular feature is noteworthy. No separate department of biography is given. Under the subject of science, for example, we find reference to Benjamin Franklin, the discoverer of electricity; under invention reference to Morse, the inventor of the telegraph, and to Edison, the inventor of the phonograph. We are referred to Geo. W. Goethals in connection with the Panama canal, to Homer in connection with Greek literature, to Baron Strathcona in Canadian history, all important figures in the world's history down to the present day. Thus the biographical characters are associated or interwoven with their particular fields of activity.

The survey of ancient, mediæval, and modern history is especially complete; the older countries are separately treated from their earliest history bringing together much information often difficult to obtain in connected form.

The literature section also is particularly useful, outlining the literatures of ancient and modern times and developing facts from the biographies of many of the world's best writers.

It will be observed that the questions under the various headings are logical, chronological where point of time is to be considered, practical, and cover sufficient material to give a thorough review of the subject treated. Often in one question reference is made to different departments thus linking together points of interest which otherwise the reader might not associate. Page numbers are frequently not in numerical order but should always be consulted in the order in which they are given.

It is the aim of the publishers that this question book serve the following purposes:

It will afford the student and the teacher a careful review of many subjects in intermediate and high school work, referring them to much valuable information not found in the ordinary textbook or in the most complete encyclopedia. Numerous questions in the various departments upon the events of the day are of particular value to the student and the teacher in securing knowledge that is up-to-date.

The literary club woman will find the history, language, and literature departments especially useful, outlining a course of study unique in points of arrangement, completeness, and up-to-dateness.

The question book should appeal to those who, having left school early, find their lack of knowledge a handicap. For commercial reasons some desire to improve, others for social reasons, yet lack the means to this end. To all such the question book affords a systematic course of home study enabling one to acquire an immense amount of practical information of inestimable value.

To build a question book is no easy task, but the publishers feel warranted in saying that this little book serves all the purposes enumerated. No aim is made to exhaust the material upon the various subjects, nor to treat all subjects found in the complete book, but rather to call attention to the vast amount of information available in this one-volume reference work, and to show what can be accomplished by diligent and careful use of The Standard Dictionary of Facts.

HOW TO USE

The Standard Question Book is founded on the comprehensive manual entitled The Standard Dictionary of Facts. It is practically a part of that reference volume, having been planned and prepared for use solely in connection with the information therein contained.

This question book, therefore, should always be studied in association with The Standard Dictionary of Facts in which will be found the answers to the questions. At this point it is important to remember that no other single source of information will furnish all of the answers to these questions. While about seven thousand are specially classified for study in this question book, The Standard Dictionary of Facts will answer in the neighborhood of a hundred thousand similar questions.

How to Study. The first necessary step is to get at the start the clearest and most definite idea possible as to what The Standard Dictionary of Facts actually contains. The second necessary step is to learn how to find any desired item of information with ease and speed.

Both of the foregoing are best accomplished by a careful reading of the Preface, pages 3 and 4 of this volume, and the Publishers' Preface, page 3, and How to Use, page 6, in The Standard Dictionary of Facts, supplemented by a little practice in using the Index and in referring to some of the alphabetical lists given at the beginning of the Index, page 867.

Suppose that one desires to acquire more information concerning the geography of Europe. First turn to the index to this book, page 155. Here one will find a list of more than a hundred important subjects, alphabetically arranged and cross-referenced, all of which are given special treatment in this question book.

Opposite the subject "Geography," which one will find among the other subjects in alphabetical order, are the figures "115-130." These figures indicate the pages where the whole subject of geography is treated. But under the head of geography one at once notices several subheads or subdivisions, beginning with "Africa." Glancing down this list of subheads, which is likewise arranged alphabetically, one soon finds "Europe," the subdivision desired. Opposite "Europe" are the figures "122-127" telling the pages on which European geography is treated. If, however, one should look for Europe first instead of geography, one would immediately find under "Europe" the subhead "Geography" with reference to pages "122-127." This illustrates how carefully all subjects treated are indexed.

Turning to the section indicated by the page numbers, one finds about five pages filled with important questions, the answers to which will furnish a good working knowledge of the geography of the whole continent of Europe. The figures following the questions indicate the pages in The Standard Dictionary of Facts where concise and accurate answers may be found. In a like manner the questions on all of the other subjects treated may be easily found and studied.

TABLE OF CONTENTS

HISTORY

ANCIENT — ENGLISH — UNITED STATES — CANADA — CONTINENTAL EUROPE—MEXICO—SOUTH AMERICA—ASIATIC COUNTRIES..11-68

LANGUAGE

CAPITALS—PUNCTUATION—CORRECT USE OF WORDS—LETTER WRITING—HIGHER ENGLISH............................69-80

LITERATURE

ANCIENT — ORIENTAL — GREEK — LATIN — MODERN EUROPEAN—ENGLISH—AMERICAN...............................81-114

GEOGRAPHY

NORTH AMERICA—SOUTH AMERICA—EUROPE—ASIA—AFRICA—GENERAL..115-130

GOVERNMENT

UNITED STATES—EUROPEAN COUNTRIES—ASIA—CENTRAL AMERICA—SOUTH AMERICA................................131-138

INDUSTRY—INVENTION—COMMERCE

IRON AND STEEL—IMPORTS—EXPORTS—SHIPPING—MANUFACTURING...139-142

SCIENCE—EDUCATION—FINE ARTS

ELECTRICITY—ENGINEERING—PHYSIOLOGY—COLLEGES AND UNIVERSITIES—SCULPTURE—PAINTING—MUSIC..............143-146

NATURAL HISTORY

MAMMALS—BIRDS—FISHES—FRUITS—FLOWERS—MINERALS—PRECIOUS STONES.....................................147-150

MISCELLANY

GENERAL INFORMATION—POINTS OF INTEREST—ORIGIN AND MEANING OF NAMES—ARITHMETIC—PARCEL POST—RED CROSS. 151-154

ANCIENT HISTORY

In studying human progress what two kinds of knowledge are
considered?.. 54

State the distinction between prehistoric times and historic times. 54

Into what two parts is the Prehistoric Period divided? Name
important achievements which preceded the invention of
writing.. 54

Name ten economic plants which were among the first to be placed
under cultivation. Mention ten important animals domesti-
cated before the dawn of history............................ 54

With the peoples of what regions does the earliest recorded history
begin? At approximately what dates?.................... 54

How must all assigned dates at the beginning of history be regarded? 54

Mention the names of five of the world's lost cities. Tell by
whom and when each was founded and how and when each
was destroyed...128-130

What are five of the notable wars of history? During what years
did each occur? Name the chief leaders and some of the
most notable battles of each war.....................138-139

What was the earliest known nation?........................ 43

EGYPT

What characters were used for the earliest Egyptian writing?.... 282

What is the Rosetta stone? When was it discovered?.......378, 282

Who is the author of the list of Egyptian kings which is still
used? Into how many dynasties does he divide them?..... 43

By whom was the Egyptian monarchy founded? What was its
capital?..43, 54

What are the dates assigned to Menes by different chronolo-
gists? Why do they vary?............................... 43

Describe the pyramids. When was the great pyramid built?.... 561

When was the city of Thebes founded? Distinguish Egyptian
Thebes from Thebes in Greece........................... 161

When was geometry used in Egypt? Give the date of a treatise
on geometry...55, 282

Who were the shepherd kings? When did they conquer Egypt,
and how long did they hold it?....................55, 43, 119

When were letters first used in Egypt? By whom and when was
the Egyptian alphabet invented?........................ 55

When were the temples and palaces at Thebes built?.......... 43

Describe the early Egyptian architecture.................... 511

What king was probably the Pharaoh of the exodus?.......... 43

During what period did the decay of the empire begin? 43
What does the word Pharaoh mean? 834
When were horses introduced into Egypt? 55
Give the origin of the name Egypt 55, 812
When did Shishak reign? After the death of Shishak by whom were the Egyptians conquered? 56, 43
What date is given to the first record of Egyptian sculpture? 57
When did Memphis become the capital of Egypt? 57
What great canal was begun in 610 B. C.? 57
In what year was Nebuchadnezzar's invasion of Egypt? 57
At what time and under what ruler did Egypt become a Persian province? 43
Give the date of Alexander's conquest of Egypt 43, 60
By whom and in what year was Alexandria founded? When was it destroyed? 128, 60
After whose death did Ptolemy take the throne? 43
What were the characteristics of the reign of the Ptolemies, and what name was applied to that period? 43, 60
Name a great canal built in Egypt 267 B. C. 61
Name the first lighthouse on record 61, 849
Who was Cleopatra, and what did her influence accomplish for Egypt? 420, 43, 63
What became of the Alexandrian library? How many books did it contain? 63, 684
Who conquered Egypt in 47 B. C.? 63
Upon whose downfall did Egypt pass to Rome? Give the date. 43, 63
Describe religious conditions in Egypt following the Roman conquest 43-44
Name a celebrated Egyptian astronomer and geographer 65, 478
When Rome was divided into eastern and western empires, of which empire did Egypt become a province? 44
Who were Osiris, Isis, Horus, and Apis? 325-338
What city was called the city of a hundred gates? What deity was especially worshiped in that city? 161
What are obelisks? For what purpose were they erected? 550

CHINA AND JAPAN

Why is it difficult to state facts about the early history of China?. 35
Name six plants cultivated in China 2700 B. C. still of great importance in agriculture 55
At what time was silk culture in China established? 55
When did the Shang dynasty begin? 55
What is known of the Chow dynasty and when did it begin? 35, 56

For how long has the mariner's compass been known to the Chinese?... 56

Who was Confucius? During whose reign was he born?....422, 35

From what dynasty did China take its name?................. 35

When was the great wall of China built, what was its purpose, and what is its length?...............................35, 817

How early was the art of printing known in China?............ 61

In what country was paper invented? Give the date.......... 62

When was Buddhism introduced into China?................... 35

What Roman emperor sent ambassadors to China?.......... 65

Name the forms of government through which Japan successively passed... 124

How many centuries of unbroken reign does the Japanese empire claim?..................................... 124

Who was the fabled first mikado and what was his descent?..... 124

From what time does the authentic history of Japan date?...... 124

Name a conquest personally made by the empress in 270 A. D... 124

From what country did Japan receive the Confucian classics?.. 317

What is the signification of the word Japan?.................. 822

CHALDEA, ASSYRIA, BABYLON

Who made Babylon preeminent? Mention his achievements.... 55

Where was the kingdom of Assyria?........................... 21

When and by whom was Nineveh built?....................... 55

When was the Assyrian empire established?...................21, 55

Name the oldest Chaldean book.............................. 281

At what time did the Babylonian decline begin?............... 281

Give the date of the second Assyrian dynasty.................. 55

Who were the most famous rulers of Assyria?................. 21

What period witnessed the revival of learning in Assyria?....... 281

Who was Sardanapalus?....................................57, 21

What size was attained by the library at Nineveh?............. 281

When was Assyria united to Babylon?........................ 21

Who was Nebuchadnezzar? When did he capture Jerusalem and when did he invade Egypt?...........................57, 470

What eclipse was observed at Babylon in 721 B. C.?............ 57

At what time and by what nation was the final conquest of Babylon accomplished?................................. 58

How long did the city of Babylon exist?...................... 128

THE HEBREWS

What dates are usually accepted for the birth and the death of Abraham?... 55

Who was Joseph? When was he sold into Egypt?..........452, 55

When was Joseph viceroy of Egypt?...................... 119

Give the date of the death of Jacob. The death of Joseph..... 55

What does the name Israel mean and to whom was it applied?.122, 822

Give the principal events in the life of Moses. What education
did he receive?.....................................468, 282

What is the date of the exodus from Egypt? The date of the
law from Sinai?...................................... 55

What position did Joshua occupy after the death of Moses?..... 452

When did Saul become king of Israel? When did he die?....... 56

Give the principal facts in the life of David and the dates of his
birth and death...................................425, 56

For how many years and at what period was Solomon king?..... 56

State some important facts concerning Solomon's life.......... 489

Describe Solomon's temple................................. 160

What is meant by the revolt of the Ten Tribes? When did it
occur? What new kingdoms were formed from the Hebrew
tribes?...56, 122

Give the names of the Ten Tribes, their population, and the
causes of their revolt.................................... 122

When and why did Jeroboam establish idolatry?.............56, 123

By what conquest did the kingdom of Israel come to an end?
Give the date.......................................57, 123

How did the title Jews come into use?.....................122, 125

After Nineveh was united to Babylon in what kingdom were the
Israelites captive?...................................... 125

Where did Daniel prophesy? Why was he in that city?......125, 424

By whom was Babylonia conquered in 538 B. C.?............. 58

What did Cyrus do for the Jews?..........................58, 125

When was Persia conquered by Alexander the Great?........... 60

Trace the history of the Jews under the Macedonian empire..... 125

Of what country did Judea become a province in 63 B. C.?...... 125

Who was Caligula? Why did he persecute the Jews?.........125, 146

By whom were the Jews banished from Rome?................ 125

What did the Jews suffer under Titus?....................... 125

When was Jerusalem founded and when was it destroyed?...... 129

What is meant by the final desolation of Judea?............... 125

PHENICIA AND PERSIA

Where was ancient Phenicia?................................ 557

According to tradition, who introduced the Phenician alphabet
into ancient Greece?...........................283, 326, 557

By whom was Carthage founded?............................ 56

14

With whom did the king of Tyre form an alliance in 1000 B. C.?.   56

Upon what great building were Phenician workmen employed?. 557

Who first circumnavigated Africa?............................   57

What Persian ruler invaded Phenicia and captured Tyre?.......57, 58

What country received the Phenician alphabet about 500 B. C.?.   58

On what continents were Phenician colonies planted?........... 557

For what knowledge were the Phenicians noted?............... 557

Where was the original country of Persia?.................... 141

By whom was the Persian empire founded? Of what countries
    was it composed?......................................58, 141

Who was Cambyses? How did he extend the empire?........415, 141

Why was the battle of Marathon of especial importance? Name
    the leaders..   22

What conquests were made by Darius?....................... 141

Who was Xerxes? What death did he meet?.................   58

Name the commander of the Persian army at Thermopylæ.
    Give facts about the battle............................... 161

When was the royal family of Persia poisoned?...............   59

At what time were the Greek cities of Asia tributary to Persia?.   59

How was Persian civilization affected as a result of the battle of
    Arbela?...   22

Name the commanders at the battle of Arbela. What nation
    thereafter controlled Persia?...........................22, 60

When and how long was Persia tributary to Parthia?..........   60

Who was Zoroaster? Where and how long did his religion pre-
    vail? State its effect upon the Greeks.................504, 278

Who are the Parsees? What is their belief? How do they
    dispose of their dead?................................278, 719

What style of writing was used by the early Persians? Upon
    what material did they prefer to write?................... 281

GREECE

Why are both the history and the literature of the ancient Greeks
    obscure?...116, 283

When was Athens founded? Who was Cecrops?.............55, 327

Give the dates of the founding of Corinth and Sparta...........   55

Who was Cadmus? What alphabet did he introduce into Greece?
    ....283, 326

When and where were the first Olympic games held? What
    were these games?....................................55, 832

Mention the first naval expedition on record...................   55

Who was Jason? Who were the argonauts? What was the
    golden fleece?.......................................325-333

Who was Apollo? When was the temple of Apollo at Delphi built?..325, 55

When and by whom were masts and sails for the use of ships invented?.. 56

What was the cause of the Trojan war?...................... 165

Give the supposed dates, the leading battle, and the chief leaders of the Trojan war.............................56, 138, 130

Who was Agamemnon? Hector?........................324, 331

Tell what is known about Homer........................... 446

Give the theme of Homer's Iliad. The theme of the Odyssey...363, 373

Who was Ulysses? What part did he play in the Trojan war?.. 342

Tell how the Greeks captured Troy in the Trojan war.......... 165

Where was the Peloponnesus?............................... 556

What is meant by the Heraclidæ?............................ 331

Who reformed the constitution of Sparta?................... 56

When and by whom were gold and silver first coined?......... 56

What boats were used by the Corinthians in the 8th century B. C.? 57

When was the Greek city of Syracuse founded? What is the origin of the name?...................................57, 842

When did the Messenian wars occur?......................116, 138

Between whom was the first sea fight on record?.............57, 116

Who was Draco? When was the Draconian code formulated?.. 428

Who were the seven sages of Greece? When did they flourish?. 116

When did Solon's code come into use in Athens?.............. 57

Mention three noted battles of the Perso-Grecian war. Which of these is one of the decisive battles of the world's history?..138, 116, 22

Give the dates of the following battles: Marathon, Thermopylæ, Salamis...58, 116

Who was the leader of the Greeks at the battle of Thermopylæ? Of what country was he king? Give result of battle..161, 116

Give facts about Sparta. What position did Sparta occupy in the 6th century B. C.?.................................. 158

When was a school of sculpture opened at Athens? The first public library founded at Athens?....................... 58

Who was Minerva? What was the Greek name for Minerva? What Grecian city is said to have received its name from Minerva?.. 335

When was the temple of Minerva built? Where was it?........ 555

When was Pericles prominent in the affairs of Athens? What great building was erected during his administration?....58, 555

Describe the Parthenon. What great Greek sculptor superintended its erection? What was its style of architecture?.555, 476

16

Name three orders of Greek architecture. In what age did Grecian architecture attain its greatest perfection?........ 511

What is meant by the Acropolis?............................ 797

Who were the principal Greek writers during the "golden age of Pericles"?... 201

Who was Phidias? Name some statues which he executed.... 476

When was the Peloponnesian war? Name the chief leaders and the cause of the war...................................138, 158

Who was the historian of the Peloponnesian war? Give facts about him...284, 494

Trace the alternating supremacy of Sparta and Athens........ 158

When was Thebes predominant in the affairs of Greece?.......59, 116

Who was Philip of Macedon? When did he subdue Sparta?..476, 59

What were the Philippics of Demosthenes?.................... 426

What position as an orator did Demosthenes hold? What obstacles did he overcome?.............................. 426

Who instituted the Macedonian phalanx?....................59, 476

When and by whom was Thebes destroyed?.................60, 130

In what war was the battle of Arbela? Give the leaders of the battle and the result...............................138, 22, 60

Why is the battle of Arbela of particular importance? Give the date.. 22

Give a brief account of the life of Alexander the Great......... 395

Name two countries that were conquered by Alexander the Great. In what year did he establish the Macedonian monarchy?... 60

In what year did the Grecian cities revolt from Macedonia? Who became regent of Greece?........................... 60

By whom was the first work on mechanics written and in what year?.. 60

Who was Aristotle? Of what great teacher was he a pupil?..... 399

What was the Achæan league? When did Athens join it?......9, 61

What caused the Achæan war?.............................. 9

When did Greece become a Roman province?.................. 62

Give the meaning of "laconic".............................. 365

Give an account of the legendary achievements of Hercules.... 331

Why has Sparta no imposing ruins?.......................... 158

Who was Herodotus?....................................... 445

State some facts in the life of Plato. What great philosopher was the teacher of Plato?............................477, 284

What was the fate of Socrates?.............................. 489

What is the theme of Xenophon's Anabasis?................284, 504

What celebrated Greek mathematician lived about 300 B. C.?.60, 431

Who was Plutarch?.. 477

Describe the Colossus at Rhodes.......................... 809

What are the Elgin marbles?.............................. 813

What is the sculpture known as the Laocoön group? Where
is it now?.. 333

Describe the mythology of the ancient Greeks. Explain how
they worshiped these deities.......................... 323

Who were the following: Zeus, Poseidon, Aphrodite, Dionysus,
Hermes? 325-342

ROME
Legendary Age

What is the mythical connection of Æneas with the founding of
the Roman empire?.................................... 343

When and by whom was Alba Longa built?.................. 56

Give the year in which Romulus became king of Alba Longa.
The year in which he was supposedly murdered...........56, 57

In what year was Rome founded? By whom?...........57, 567, 378

What change was made in the Roman calendar in 710 B. C.?... 57

Give in order three important kings of Rome from 672 B. C.
to 578 B. C.. 57

What is the Cloaca Maxima, and under what ruler was it constructed?.. 809

What was the Roman forum?.............................. 110

Explain the Circus Maximus.............................. 808

Who was Servius Tullius? When did he die?.............. 567

How large had Rome become in the time of Servius Tullius?.. 567

Name the seven hills of Rome............................ 567

What great building of ancient Rome stood on the Palatine
hill?.. 566

Under what ruler was the coining of money begun at Rome?.... 57

When were the Tarquins expelled from Rome? What uprising
of the people took place in Athens a year earlier?......... 58

Who were Janus, Juno, Jupiter, Mars, Minerva?.............333-335

Who was Vesta? What were the Lares? The Penates? The
Manes?...334-342

The Republic

What great change in the government of Rome took place in
509 B. C.?.. 58

When was the Capitol at Rome finished? The temple of Minerva
built?.. 58

In what year were tribunes of the people first chosen?.......... 58

Where is the Tarpeian rock and what is its history?............ 159
When was Cincinnatus made dictator?......................59, 420
Who were the decemviri and what did they do?............... 39
When were the laws of the twelve tables adopted?............. 59
In what year was Rome destroyed by the Gauls?............. 59
What civil strife took place in 376 B. C.? Who was made the
    first plebeian consul?..................................... 59
When were military tribunes abolished?..................... 59
When did the Samnite war begin? How long did it continue?. 59
When was the Appian way constructed? Where was it?.......60, 800
When was the sun dial at Rome erected?..................... 60
In what year did Rome become mistress of all Italy?........... 61
Give the dates of beginning and ending of the Punic wars..... 138
Who was Hannibal? What had he to do with the second Punic
    war?..442, 61
When did Macedonia become a Roman province?............. 62
Name the principal events between the second and third Punic
    wars..61-62
During what war did Greece become a Roman province? What
    great cities were taken by Rome in that year?............. 62
When did Spain pass under Roman rule?..................... 62
Who was Caius Gracchus? When did he become tribune?.....439, 62
Sketch the life of Cornelia, "mother of the Gracchi"........... 422
Give the dates of the Jugurthine war and the names of the leaders.
    State facts about Jugurtha...........................138, 452
What was the Roman social war and what was the result?.... 138
Who was made perpetual dictator of Rome as a result of his
    successes in war?...................................... 63
Give the dates, the leaders, and the important battles of the
    Mithridatic war.. 138
Who were the gladiators? What was Cicero's reason for approv-
    ing of their contests?................................. 116
Who were the chief leaders of the Gladiatorial war and when
    did it occur?....................................138, 423, 489
Who was Catiline? When and by whom was his conspiracy
    discovered?..417, 63
Outline the events of Cicero's life........................... 419
What is a triumvirate? Name the members of the first Roman
    triumvirate..165, 63
Sketch briefly the life of Julius Cæsar, giving dates of birth
    and death.. 414
When did Cæsar become dictator of Rome?................... 63
For whom was the month of July named?................... 823

When did Cæsar invade Britain?............................ 63
What became of Crassus and Pompey?...................... 63
Who succeeded Cæsar as master of Rome?.................. 63
Name the members of the second Roman triumvirate.......... 63
Give briefly the life of Mark Antony. By whom and in what
    battle was he defeated?...............................462, 63
Sketch the life of Cleopatra................................ 420
Name the wars in which Rome was engaged before the beginning
    of the Christian era..................................... 138
What aqueducts were built during the period of the republic?... 510

The Empire

In what year did the republic of Rome become a monarchy?
    What was the population of Rome at that time?........... 63
What titles were conferred upon Octavius by the Roman senate? 63
How long did Augustus (Octavius) rule? What was the charac-
    ter of his reign?.....................................146, 401
For what writings were Sallust, Virgil, Horace, and Livy noted?
    Compare the time in which they lived with the date of
    Augustus' reign.................................447-497, 146
For whom was the month of August named?.................. 801
In what year did Augustus correct the calendar?.............. 64
In what year did the birth of Christ occur?................... 64
Mention the principal events in the reign of Augustus, noting
    particularly all conquests made.........................63-64
Describe the Pantheon. When was it built?...............554, 566
Which one of the decisive battles of history took place in 9 A. D.? 22
Under which of the Roman emperors did the crucifixion of Christ
    take place?...64, 146
Name the Roman emperors from 14 A. D. to 96 A. D.......... 146
For what qualities were Caligula and Nero noted?........64, 415, 470
During whose reign was the city of Rome burned? What great
    palace was built in the same year?.....................64, 817
How did the streets of the rebuilt city compare with those of
    the old city of Rome?................................... 566
Who first persecuted the Christians?........................ 64
State some facts about Titus. What were the baths of Titus?..64, 566
What volcanic eruption caused the destruction of Pompeii?
    Who was emperor of Rome at the time?...........558, 576, 146
What is the arch of Titus? The Colosseum?..........800, 809, 566
Who were the five good emperors?.......................... 146
During whose reign was the Roman empire at its greatest extent?. 65
State five facts about the life of Marcus Aurelius Antoninus.... 401

When did the period of military despotism begin?............. 146

What kind of ruler was Septimius Severus? Mention three
    events of his reign.................................... 65

What rights did Caracalla grant the people of Rome? What
    was the character of his reign?.....................65, 415

What is meant by the thirty tyrants of Rome?................ 161

Who was Aurelian? When did he rule Rome and what con-
    quests did he make?................................401, 65

What was Diocletian's form of government?.................. 65

Trace the persecution of the Christians under the Roman em-
    perors..64-65

What action did Constantius take in regard to the persecution
    of the Christians?..................................... 65

Describe the catacombs.................................... 781

Who was the first Christian emperor?....................... 65

What is the story of Constantine's conversion to Christianity?.. 422

Give the earlier name of the city of Constantinople. Why
    was it changed?....................................... 809

By what decree was Christianity made the state religion?...... 422

What is the arch of Constantine?.......................800, 566

Who was Julian the Apostate? What attempt particularly
    distinguished his reign?................................ 452

Under what rulers was the Roman empire divided?............ 65

Upon the death of Valens who succeeded to the eastern empire?.. 65

When did Theodosius become emperor of the East and the
    West?.. 66

Between whom and in what year was the Roman empire finally
    divided?... 66

Who where the Goths?..................................... 116

When was Rome sacked by Alaric?.......................66, 394

How many years elapsed between the sack of Rome by the
    Gauls and the sack of Rome by Alaric?.................59, 66

By whom and in what year were public schools established in
    Rome?... 66

Mention the conquests made and the Roman provinces acquired
    by foreign tribes between 410 A. D. and 433 A. D.......... 66

Who were the Huns?...................................... 119

Give three facts from the life of Attila. By whom was the city
    of Venice founded?.................................... 401

Sketch the life of Genseric. When did he sack Rome?........ 436

Who was the last of the Roman emperors of the West?........ 147

What king was the final conqueror of western Rome?.......... 66

How many years elapsed between the founding of the city of
    Rome and the fall of the western empire?................. 66

Mention some great Roman temples and the rulers by whom
    they were built.. 566

Describe the bridges of ancient Rome....................... 778

Who were the augurs? Distinguish between auguries and
    auspices...21-22

When was the first library opened at Rome? How many years
    earlier was the first library opened at Athens?............62, 58

What were the sacred groves at Rome?...................... 330

Give an account of the Flaminian way. Describe the Appian way.
    Compare these two examples of Roman road building.....815, 800

Quote the words of the king of Parthia when Crassus, of the
    first Roman triumvirate, was killed...................... 423

State the customs connected with the temple of Janus.......... 333

For what reason did Cæsar build a temple to Venus?........... 566

What became of Brutus after the assassination of Cæsar?..... 412

When was the circus of Romulus built? How do its ruins com-
    pare with those of other circuses?....................... 808

Where is Fiesole? For what is it noted?..................... 815

In what year was the arch of Constantine built? To com-
    memorate what event?................................. 800

Describe the sculpture known as "The Dying Gaul". Of what
    school of sculpture is it a specimen?...................... 786

When was the capitol at Rome destroyed by lightning?......... 65

In what year was Rome entirely surrounded with a wall?....... 65

When was the city of Pisa founded? What was its condition
    during the empire?..................................... 558

Describe the ancient city of Pompeii as disclosed by excavations.
    What was the size of the houses and of what were they mainly
    built? Who usually occupied the ground floors of the
    dwellings?..558-559

By whom was the city of Cologne founded?................... 526

From what century does the cathedral of Ravenna date?....... 563

ENGLISH HISTORY

By what name was Britain known to the Phenicians?.......... 804
How did Britain receive its name?........................... 804
In search of what metal did the Carthaginians visit Britain?.... 58
From what country did most of the gold antiquities of British history come?... 121
Name two metals used for coins in Britain before the Roman invasion.. 656
What was the original name of Scotland?..................... 840
By what name is Ireland mentioned by the early writers?....... 121
To what people did the early British owe their language?....... 185
Who were the Druids?....................................... 42
What aboriginal race still inhabits some parts of Wales?...... 577

Roman Period

When did the Romans first invade Britain and under what leader?... 63
Under what governor was Roman power established in Britain?.64, 394
For what purpose was the wall of Antoninus built? How far did Agricola penetrate into Scotland at that time?.......846, 154
Give the extent of the wall built by the Roman emperor Hadrian...65, 818
In what British city was Constantine the Great proclaimed emperor of Rome?..................................... 422
What was the capital of Roman Britain?...................... 581
Name five English words of Latin origin which date from the Roman occupation of Britain............................ 185
Give five English words of Latin origin introduced when the Britons were converted to Christianity.................... 185
What was the state of agriculture in Britain during the Roman period?.. 647
When was Britain abandoned by the Romans?................ 66
Why was Rome unable to defend Britain against the Scots and Picts?.. 45
How long did the Romans occupy Britain?.................... 647
State some facts regarding the history of Ireland before the sixth century.. 121
When did St. Patrick undertake to convert the natives of Ireland? 121

Coming of the Saxons

After the withdrawal of the Romans to whom did the Britons
appeal for aid?... 45

Who were Hengest and Horsa? What assistance did they
render the Britons?.....................................45, 66

Why did the Saxons remain in Britain? What part of the
island did they conquer?................................. 45

Mention three tribes of Teutonic invaders..................... 45

What part of the island was occupied by the Angles?.......... 45

Which of the Teutonic invaders formed the first settlement?
Where?.. 45

What was the witenagemot?...............................67, 847

Trace the development of the Saxon heptarchy. Under what
ruler were these Saxon kingdoms united?.................. 45

Give the origin of the word Saxon...........................840

Describe the development of Christianity through the influence
of Ethelbert, king of Kent............................. 45

By whom was St. Augustine sent to preach Christianity in Britain
in 597 A. D.?... 401

When and by whom was St. Paul's church in London founded?. 68

Who published the first code of laws in Britain?.............. 68

In what part of Britain did literature have its beginning?..... 297

Anglo-Saxon Kings

Who was the first king of England?......................... 150

Name the Anglo-Saxon kings in the order of succession. How
long did they rule?..................................... 150

What is the origin of the word England? When was the name
applied to Britain as a whole? How was the word at first
spelled?...813, 45

Give three facts which distinguish the reign of Alfred the Great.70, 395

Who was Dunstan? What power did he exert?...............70, 46

Where was Glastonbury abbey?............................. 816

Mention the principal changes brought about during the reign
of the Anglo-Saxon kings............................... 46

Danish Kings

Who succeeded the Anglo-Saxons in 1017?.................... 150

Name the Danish kings in order of their reign. How long did
they rule?.. 150

What countries besides England were ruled by Canute?......46, 72

Characterize the reign of Canute........................... 415

Saxon Kings

Under what king was the Saxon power restored in 1042?......46, 150

Name the Saxon kings and state how long they ruled........... 150

What was the character of the reign of Edward the Confessor?.46, 429

What abbey was built during the reign of Edward the Confessor?. 579

Norman Kings

Who was the first Norman king? What was his claim to the throne?..150, 502

By what battle did William the Conqueror gain the English throne, and on what date was he crowned?................ 502

What was the character of the reign of William the Conqueror?. 502

Name the Norman kings. Give period of their rule............ 150

What is meant by the feudal system? When was it introduced into England?.......................................110, 74

What was the Domesday book?.............................. 353

Describe the tower of London. For what was it used in early times?... 163

By what name was William II commonly known? Give meaning of the name...46, 838

What events characterize the reign of Henry I?..............46, 445

To whom did Henry I will the crown?....................... 46

How did Stephen attain to the English throne?............... 46

What were the tournaments and when were they introduced into England?... 163

What was the effect of the Norman conquest on the English language?...185–186

The Plantagenets

Who was the first Plantagenet king? Explain his right to the throne..46–47

Name the Plantagenet kings in order of succession. How long did they reign? Why were they called Plantagenets?.150-151, 835

What were the inherited possessions of Henry II?.............. 47

Give the most important events of the reign of Henry II........ 445

What religious controversy arose between Henry II and Thomas à Becket?...................................47, 404

Mention the circumstances in connection with the death of Thomas à Becket...................................... 404

In whose reign was Ireland added to England?...........76, 150, 445

By what name was Richard I popularly known?..............151, 47

What were the crusades? Who led the third crusade?..........38, 47

Who attempted to take Richard I's throne?................... 47

Outline the principal events in the reign of John............... 47

What was the Magna Charta? In whose reign was it signed?
Give the date.... ....827, 47

What circumstances led to the granting of the Magna Charta?. 47

By whom was the Magna Charta declared void?.............. 47

What was the character of the reign of Henry III?............. 47

When was the so-called "mad parliament"?..................47, 76

To whom is the origin of the house of commons due? In what
battle was he slain?..................................... 47

What was the cause of the battle of Lewes? What was its effect
upon Henry III's reign?..............................47, 445

In whose reign was Westminster abbey as it now stands begun?. 579

In whose reign did the first regular parliament meet and of what
did it consist?...47, 76

What nickname was given Edward I?....................... 429

When was Wales annexed to England? Give meaning of word
Wales...47, 76, 846

Name two contestants for the throne of Scotland during the
reign of Edward I.....................................76, 429

What part did Edward I take in the struggle for the Scottish
throne?...429, 47

What legislative reforms took place in the reign of Edward I?. 47

In what year was Robert Bruce proclaimed king of Scotland?... 78

In whose reign did Scotland gain her independence? By what
battle? Give date...................................... 47

Sketch briefly the life of Robert Bruce........................ 412

What title was first conferred upon Edward II?.............. 429

What was the fate of Edward II?..........................48, 429

Contrast the reign of Edward III with that of Edward II.......48, 47

Give the cause of the hundred years' war. How long did it
last? Who was king of England when it began?........118, 151

Give an account of the battle of Crécy. Name two other battles
won by Edward III..................................527, 48

Upon what condition did Edward III receive the west of France?. 48

Who succeeded Edward III? What was his age at the time of his
accession?.. 151

What was Wat Tyler's insurrection?......................... 48

Under what circumstances was Richard II deposed? From what
noted house was his successor chosen?...................48, 151

During the reign of what Plantagenet king was the scene of
"Ivanhoe" laid?....................................... 363

About what time was gunpowder first used by the English?..... 78

Name two inventions ascribed to Roger Bacon................. 402

Mention three noted English writers of the 14th century........ 298

House of Lancaster

Name the kings of the house of Lancaster, and give period of reign.. 151

Who was the rightful heir to the throne at the time of the accession of Henry IV?................................. 48

From what Plantagenet king was Henry IV descended?...... 151

Who were the Lollards?....................................48, 127

Under whose reign were heretics first burned in England?.... 48

What foreign crown was claimed by Henry V?.................48, 78

In what war was the battle of Agincourt? By whom was it won? Give date.......................................138, 78

What were the provisions of the treaty of Troyes?............. 48

How old was Henry VI when he was crowned king?..........151, 48

Give an account of the life of Joan of Arc. How did she aid France in the hundred years' war?...................399, 22, 81

Describe Cade's rebellion..................................... 33

What was the only French possession retained by the English at the close of the hundred years' war?.................118, 138

Give the cause of the wars of the roses. Why were they so called? 48

For how many years did the wars of the roses continue? Name the principal battles fought...........................48, 138

House of York

Who was the first king of the house of York? How did he obtain the throne?....................................151, 48

Name the kings of the house of York and give the period of their reign.. 151

What influence had the earl of Warwick upon the reign of Edward IV?...498, 80

What term is sometimes applied to the earl of Warwick?........ 498

How long did Edward V reign? What were the circumstances of his death?...48, 429

How did Richard III obtain the crown?.....................48, 480

What battle closed the wars of the roses? What English king was killed in this battle?...................................48, 480

Who published the first printed book in England?...........299, 417

House of Tudor

By the accession of what English king were the houses of Lancaster and York united? He was the first of what line of kings?...48, 151

Why were the Tudor kings so called?......................... 165

Name the Tudor kings in order of succession. How long did they rule?.. 151

What was the "star chamber"? In whose reign was it revived?. 158

What was Poyning's law and when was it passed?............. 121

How many times was Henry VIII married?.................. 49

Who was Cardinal Wolsey?................................ 503

What was the most important event in the reign of Henry VIII? What was its cause?...............................49, 445

How did Henry VIII secure for himself the position as head of the English church?..................................... 49

What king of Scotland was killed in the battle of Flodden? In what year?....................................154, 80

What king of England assumed the title of king of Ireland?.... 121

Name the three children of Henry VIII who succeeded him to the throne...151, 49

Sketch briefly the reign of Edward VI. How long did he reign?.49, 151

What led to the execution of Lady Jane Grey? In whose reign was she beheaded?...............................49, 82, 151

What were the religious conditions during the reign of Mary?...82, 463

Who was Thomas Cranmer? Nicholas Ridley?.............423, 480

Explain the claim of Mary, Queen of Scots, to the English throne at the time Elizabeth became queen...................... 463

Whose daughter was Mary, Queen of Scots?.................463, 154

What was the Spanish armada and when was it destroyed?.....21, 82

What were the achievements of Sir Walter Raleigh during the reign of Elizabeth? What colony did he name for the queen?... 479

In what year was the first newspaper published in England?..... 82

Mention three writers of the Elizabethan age................. 299

During whose reign was Mary, Queen of Scots, beheaded, and why?.. 463

Who succeeded Mary, Queen of Scots, as ruler of Scotland?..... 154

House of Stuart

What house of kings succeeded the Tudor line?................ 151

Name the kings of the house of Stuart? How long did the Stuarts reign?.. 151

Of what country was James I already king when he became king of England? What countries were thus united under one sovereign?...............................49, 82, 449, 590

What is meant by the "divine right of kings"? What influence had this claim upon the reign of James I?................42, 49

Who was the head of the conspiracy known as the gunpowder
    plot? Explain the plot.................................... 117
When and where was the first English settlement made in Amer-
    ica? For what English king was the colony named?.168, 82, 822
Give the date of the King James version of the Bible........... 300
Upon what charge was Sir Walter Raleigh executed?.......... 479
In what year did the Pilgrims sail for America? Give name of
    the vessel... 82
What province of Ireland was seized by James I? By whom
    was it settled?.. 122
Who discovered the circulation of the blood? Name the king
    of England at that time...........................82, 151
Sketch the trouble between parliament and the king in the reign
    of Charles I......................................49, 418
By what parliament was the "star chamber" abolished? In what
    respect did it violate the Magna Charta?................ 158
Mention the leading battles and chief leaders of the English
    civil war... 139
What were Cromwell's ironsides?............................. 122
Sketch the principal facts in the life of Oliver Cromwell....... 423
In what manner did Cromwell secure the execution of Charles I? 423
When and where was Charles I beheaded?..................... 418
What was the result of the English civil war between king and
    parliament?... 139
Under what leader was the commonwealth established?........84, 49
Describe the political conditions which existed during the early
    years of the commonwealth............................ 49
Mention two battles in which Cromwell defeated the Scottish
    royalists.. 423
When and how did Cromwell dissolve the "long parliament"? ..423, 49
What title was conferred upon Cromwell by "Barebone's par-
    liament"?... 49
Whom did George Monk proclaim as the successor of Oliver
    Cromwell?.. 467
In what year did the commonwealth begin? When was the
    house of Stuart restored?...........................84, 151
Who brought about the restoration of the Stuarts under Charles
    II?...418, 467
What great legislative act particularly distinguished the reign
    of Charles II?....................................418, 50, 84
Who were the covenanters? The dissenters?.................38, 709
When was the great fire in London?......................... 84
Give the characteristics of the reign of James II.............. 50

Who were the tories? The whigs?.......................... 163

By whom was James II driven from his kingdom?........... 449

By what authority did William III become king? Who ruled
jointly with him?......................................50, 151

Over whom did William III gain a victory at the battle of the
Boyne? Give date of battle............................502, 84

To whom was the term "Orangemen" applied?............... 832

In whose reign was the bank of England founded? Give date..84, 151

Mention some provisions of the "declaration of rights".......... 50

What was the "toleration act"?...........................162, 50

Explain the purpose of the grand alliance formed by William
III. What advantage did the alliance give England during Queen Anne's reign?............................... 50

State some facts about the first duke of Marlborough..........50, 463

Mention two battles won by the duke of Marlborough. Which
one of these is one of the decisive battles of the world's
history?...50, 22

When was the war of the Spanish succession? What great
fortress was taken by the English during that war?..139, 84, 533

When were England and Scotland united as The United Kingdom
of Great Britain?....................................50, 86

Give the date of the first united parliament of Great Britain.... 86

What territories did England gain by the treaty of Utrecht?..50, 165

Describe St. Paul's cathedral. When was it rebuilt and at what
cost?.. 571

Who was the architect of St. Paul's cathedral? Where is he
buried?...571, 503

Under what ruler did England adopt the "Union Jack" as the
national flag? Give the origin of the term................ 852

What progress in science was made by Sir Isaac Newton?....... 470

What name is given to the age of English literature of the period
of Queen Anne?....................................... 398

What religious persecution did John Bunyan suffer during the
reign of the Stuarts?................................. 413

House of Hanover

What house of kings succeeded the house of Stuart? Why were
they so called?....................................... 50

Name the kings of the house of Hanover. How long did the
house of Hanover rule?............................... 151

What was the south sea bubble?...........................841, 50

What influence did Sir Robert Walpole exert on the reigns of
George I and George II?............................... 50

In what wars did George II take an active part?...........50-51, 139

What treaty closed the war of the Austrian succession?........51, 164

Who was William Pitt? What important position did he hold?..477, 51

What is meant by the black hole of Calcutta?................ 777

In the reign of George II what changes were made in the calendar? 51

When was Canada formally ceded to Great Britain?........... 34

When was 'Great Britain at war with the American colonies?
What was the result of this war?........................86, 51

What led to the impeachment of Warren Hastings? In whose
reign did it occur?...............................443, 86, 151

What caused the war between England and France in 1793?.... 52

What brilliant naval victory was won by the English in 1805?.52, 88

Give some facts about Horatio Nelson. In what battle was he
killed?... 470

What were the Berlin decrees?............................... 52

Describe the battle of Waterloo. Give leaders, date, and result. 179

Of what particular importance is the battle of Waterloo?...... 22

With what country did Great Britain engage in war in 1812?.. 88

In what year was the legislative union of Great Britain and
Ireland consummated? 122

When was the spinning machine first used in England?........ 86

Give the year in which iron railways were first used in England.
Steam carriages... 88

When was gas first used for lighting the streets of London?.... 88

What important medical discovery was made by Edward Jenner?
Give date... 450

Name important inventions made by the following: Arkwright,
Crompton, Watt...............................:399-499, 668

Mention some of the reforms of the reign of George IV......... 52

What was accomplished by the reform bill of 1832?............ 52

During whose reign did Great Britain abolish negro slavery?.52, 151

Sketch briefly the main facts in the life of Queen Victoria.... 497

Of what political party was Sir Robert Peel the leader? Under
what name did he reorganize this party?.................52, 475

Upon whose recommendation and in what year were the English
corn laws repealed? In what part of the empire did severe
famine exist?..52, 90

Upon what plea did Great Britain become involved in the Crimean
war? What alliance was formed against Russia?...........52-53

Give leading battles, chief leaders, and period of the Crimean
war...139, 38

In what year was the government of India transferred to the
British crown?.. 53

Give chief events in the lives of the following: Gladstone, Disraeli,
Cecil Rhodes.....................................438, 428, 480
When was the first Atlantic cable laid?......................670, 92
In what year were the British North-American colonies united
as the Dominion of Canada?............................34, 53
Give the dates of two Irish land acts passed during Gladstone's
administration as prime minister....................... 53
Upon what queen was the title of empress of India first conferred?.53, 94
What were the causes of the Boer war? How long did it last?.53, 27-29
Mention five writers of the Victorian age of English literature.. 303

House of Saxe-Coburg

Show how the name Saxe-Coburg is applied to the successors of
Queen Victoria.. 497
Name the first king of the house of Saxe-Coburg. The present
king. When did the reign of each begin?...............151, 605
When and by whom was the name of the royal house of England
changed from Saxe-Coburg to Windsor?. 151
Who became premier of England in 1902? What policy did he
oppose in 1903?...................................53, 402
What measures were proposed by Rt. Hon. Joseph Chamberlain
in 1903?.. 417
Who succeeded Balfour as prime minister of England? In what
year?...53, 415
When did Asquith become prime minister of England? What
wage bill did he introduce?..........................53, 400
Mention two important measures of which Lloyd George is the
author... 458
In what year was the old age pension act passed? The mini-
mum wage bill?....................................53, 96
What important legislative act in behalf of Ireland was intro-
duced by Premier Asquith in 1912?..................... 122
Of what does the present British parliament consist?........... 590
Name the countries composing the United Kingdom..........534-535
When and how were Wales, Scotland, and Ireland acquired by
England?..534-535
Name the deposed kings of England.......................... 41
What ruler of England ruled the greatest number of years?..... 151

AMERICAN HISTORY

Name five Norsemen who visited America in the 10th and 11th centuries. In what early writings are accounts of their voyages found?....................................98, 168, 146

Tell what you can about Eric the Red......................431, 98

To what part of North America was the name Vinland given? What discoverer is believed to have named it? When did he land?..386, 146, 168

When and where was Christopher Columbus born? State his early occupation, the voyage of discovery he planned to make, the years of waiting, the attitude of Queen Isabella towards his project...421, 448

Give the date on which Columbus discovered America, and name the place at which he first landed. What does San Salvador mean?..421, 839

From what country did Columbus sail? What large island did he discover? How many voyages did he make?......98, 810, 421

Give an account of the voyages of John and Sebastian Cabot. What land was discovered by each? Give dates......168, 414, 98

Who was Amerigo Vespucci? What claims did he make in regard to his discoveries?............................... 396

When, for whom, and by whom was America named?........799, 396

By whom was Florida discovered? In what year? Why was the name Florida chosen?..........................98, 477, 815

Name the discoverer of the Pacific ocean. Where did he plant a colony?..98, 402

By whom was Mexico discovered? By whom was it conquered? Give details of the conquest.....:.........................98, 423

When was Panama settled? What does the name Panama mean? By whom was the city of Panama founded?..98, 833, 552

What was the nationality of Jacques Cartier? In whose name did he claim North America? Why was the gulf of St. Lawrence so named?......... ....416, 34, 839

Name a discovery made by De Soto. Give the date. How far did he explore the country?......................427, 168

Who founded the city of St. Augustine, Florida? In what year? For what historical fact is it noted?..........98, 838, 168

When was Santa Fé founded? What is the meaning of its name?. 839

Where did Sir Walter Raleigh's expedition plant a colony? In what year was this settlement made? What name was given to the territory?..............................168, 98, 179

33

What English colony did Sir Francis Drake visit? Name a
naval achievement for which he is celebrated............98, 428
For whom was the city of Raleigh named? When was it settled?. 837
Mention the first Englishman to visit Massachusetts. What
part of the coast did he discover?......................132, 98
Connect an important discovery with each of these dates: 1492,
1497, 1534.. 98
Name the oldest European settlement on the American continent.
The oldest in the United States. The oldest permanent
English settlement in America........................552, 168
Give the name of the first English child born in America. The
first white child born in New England................... 98

The Period of Colonization

To what company did James I grant a charter for the territory
known as Virginia? What was the extent of their territory?... 179
When did the English make their first permanent settlement at
Jamestown, Va.? Why did they call the place James-
town?..98, 822
Give an account of the life of Capt. John Smith. Of Poca-
hontas......................................489, 477, 179
By whom were the first slaves brought to Virginia? When?.. 98
When and by whom was Quebec settled? Are any Canadian
cities older than Quebec?..........................98, 562
Give the population of Virginia in 1641...................... 179
Who became governor of Virginia in 1642? What was the cause
of Bacon's rebellion? When did it occur?..............99, 179
In what year was Maryland settled? By whom? When was an
act of religious toleration passed?...................98, 168, 131
When was the city of Baltimore founded? For whom was it
named?...131, 801
What is Mason and Dixon's line? When was it adopted?.....132, 131
Trace the history of the name Carolina as applied to North and
South Carolina....................................... 806
Name the first settlement in South Carolina. Give date. Until
what date were the two Carolinas united?...............155, 99
For what is John Locke known to Americans?................ 458
Name the first settlement in Georgia. Who made it? After
whom was Georgia named?......................624, 113, 472
When and by whom was the first settlement within the state of
New Jersey made? Where? Of what state was New Jersey
originally a part?..................................135, 624

34

Explain the circumstances which led to the granting of a separate constitution for New Jersey. Why was New Jersey so named?...135, 831

When was Plymouth, Mass., founded? State the origin of its name..;.....168, 835

Tell what people settled Plymouth, from what country they came, and the name of the ship in which they sailed. Who was their leader?.............................132, 168, 98

Name the first governor of the Plymouth colony. The second..   98

Sketch the life of Miles Standish. In what way was he helpful to the Plymouth colony?................................ 490

In what historic poem by Longfellow is Priscilla a character? Tell the story of the poem................................... 376

What company sent John Endicott to America? What settlements were planted by his expedition?.................... 132

When and by whom was Salem settled? Boston? Give the origin of both names...........................168, 839, 803

Who were the first and second governors of Massachusetts colony? What influence did the second exert?...........98, 503

Why was Roger Williams banished from Massachusetts?...... 502

In what year was Harvard college founded? By whom?.98, 699, 443

By whom and where was the first printing press established in the British American colonies? In what year?.......... 98

In what part of America did King Philip's war take place? How long did it last? Give dates. Who was King Philip?...168, 476

Mention two colonies which were affected by King Philip's war...132, 146

When did Massachusetts lose her charter? When was a new charter issued? Name two colonies united in 1692....... 132

Who was at the head of the Plymouth company which made unsuccessful attempts to settle the Maine region? Between what parallels did this territory lie?........................,.. 131

When were the first two settlements made in New Hampshire? Name them..135, 168

When was Maine first set apart? To whom was its charter granted?.. 131

Why was New Hampshire so named? Maine?..............831, 827

Under the jurisdiction of what province did Maine and New Hampshire fall? When did New Hampshire become a separate province?..............................168, 131, 135

Name two countries claiming the Connecticut territory. Which finally secured it?...................................... 37

Where and by whom were the first three settlements made in Connecticut? Give dates............................... 37

By whom was the city of New Haven founded?................ **37**

Give the date of the first constitution of Connecticut. Why is this constitution worthy of special mention?...................98, 37

Tell the story of the charter oak. Where was it? Who was governor at that time? What action was he endeavoring to take?...35, 37

Give an account of the settling of Rhode Island, with date. Name the first settlement in the state. Mention three later settlements in Rhode Island.......................98, 146, 168

When did Hendrik Hudson explore the river which bears his name? By whom was he employed?..................... **135**

By whom was New York state first settled? Where? When?..135, 98

State the extent of the territory called New Netherland. Into the possession of what company did it soon pass?.......... **135**

When and by whom was Albany settled? Under what name?..168, 135

How did the Dutch acquire Manhattan island? Who was their governor at that time?................................... **135**

When did Peter Stuyvesant become governor of New Amsterdam?. **99**

On what grounds did the English claim New Netherland? How were these claims enforced?...........................135, 168

Give the date upon which New Amsterdam became New York. For whom was New York named?......................135, 168

State the nationality of the first settlers of Delaware. By whom were they driven out? To what country was Delaware next subjected?....................................... **39**

To whom did the English sell Delaware? With what state was it governed until the revolution? For whom was Delaware named?.......................................39, 811

Who colonized Pennsylvania? Give date. State five important facts concerning the settlement of Pennsylvania.........140-141

Tell some facts about William Penn. What city did he found? What does its name mean?......................475, 140, 834

Where did each of the following make explorations: Marquette? Joliet? La Salle?.................................99, 456, 130

By whom was New Orleans founded? When?...............130, 99

Name three wars between the French and the English from 1692 to 1748. What was the principal event of King George's war?.168, 99

When did the French and Indian war begin? Name six of its prominent events..................................... **168**

Who won the battle of Fort Duquesne? Give facts about the English commander...................................99, 410

Mention two generals killed in the battle of Quebec. State which army was victorious........................99, 467, 503

What country was called Acadia? Where were the Acadians taken in 1755? When was Acadia ceded to the British? 797, 99-100, **343**

By what treaty was the French and Indian war ended? To what countries did France cede Canada and Louisiana?.168, 34, **130**

When did Franklin discover electricity?.......................**86, 99**

Name in the order in which they were settled the thirteen original colonies. Give the dates of settlement of Virginia, New York, Massachusetts, Maryland......................... **624**

Mention an important event in the history of British America that occurred during 1620. Of French America. Of Spanish America.. **98**

Explain what is meant by the Mecklenburg declaration......... **132**

What were the Blue Laws? In what state and in what year were they compiled?.................................... **27**

The Revolutionary Period

Who became king of England in 1760?....................... **151**

State the sentiment of the colonies after the close of the French and Indian war. What were "writs of assistance"?....... **169**

When was the stamp act passed? Tell of its provisions and how it was received by the colonists..................... **169**

In what city did delegates assemble to resist the stamp act? Give details of the action taken by the congress........100, **169**

When was the stamp act repealed? By what other taxes was it followed?... **169**

Describe the Boston massacre. The Boston tea party........ **169**

What were the provisions of the Boston port bill?............. **169**

Give the date of the first continental congress. Where did it meet? How many colonies were represented? What action was taken?...................................... **169**

State some facts about John Hancock....................... **442**

Who warned the people of Lexington of the British attack? Describe the battle of Lexington.......................127, **480**

Give the exact date of the battle of Lexington. Tell why this battle was of so great importance..................169, 127, **100**

Mention the important conquests made by Ethan Allen..169, 396, **162**

Relate in detail the proceedings of the second continental congress... **169**

In what year was George Washington appointed commander-in-chief of the American forces?.......................100, **169**

Describe the battle of Bunker Hill...........................32, **169**

Mention an important event of March 17, 1776.............169, **519**

When and where was the declaration of independence adopted?
By whom was it written?............................100, 169
Give in substance the first, second, and last paragraphs of the
declaration of independence. Name five of the prominent
signers....................:........................599-600
When was the first United States flag unfurled? Explain the
origin of the stars and stripes. When was the flag adopted
by congress? Who called the flag "Old Glory"?....100, 789, 110
Give the history of the liberty bell.......................... 794
What was the result of the battle of Long Island? Of White
Plains? What is meant by Washington's retreat?......... 169
How did Washington spend Christmas night, 1776?............ 169
What part did each of the following take in the revolution:
Cornwallis? Lafayette? Kosciusko?...................422-455
Name an American city taken by the British forces in 1777...100, 170
Name the commanders at the battle of Saratoga. What was
the result of this battle?..........................170, 413, 436
Mention three battles of 1777 in which Gen. Burgoyne partici-
pated.. 170
Give the date of Burgoyne's surrender at Saratoga. Why is
Saratoga one of the decisive battles of history?..........170, 22
Where is Valley Forge? For what is it noted?..............845, 170
State which army was victorious at each of the following battles:
Monmouth, Savannah, Stony Point, Charleston, Camden,
King's Mountain....................................170, 11-19
Give three important facts concerning the life of Anthony
Wayne. When was the battle of Stony Point?..........499, 18
What brilliant service did Paul Jones render the American
colonists?.....................................100, 170, 452
Tell the history of Major André and Benedict Arnold...397, 399, 100
In what part of the country were most of the military operations
of 1781? Under what commander?...................... 170
Mention three battles of 1781 in the South.................... 170
What was the last battle of the revolution? Give date and
place of Cornwallis' surrender.........................170, 100
In what year were the articles of confederation adopted by the
thirteen colonies? When were they ratified? When did
they go into effect?............................100, 586, 170
In what city and in what year was the bank of North America
established? Give facts about Robert Morris.......100, 468, 652
By what treaty was the revolution closed?..................100, 164
Give an account of Shays's rebellion.......................100, 154

In what year did the constitutional convention assemble at
Philadelphia? When was the constitution adopted? When
did it become effective?.........................100, 170, 594
Show why the achievements of the following entitle them to
be ranked as noted Americans: Benjamin Franklin, Patrick
Henry, Thomas Jefferson, Samuel Adams, John Jay......394-450
In what year was the independence of the United States recognized
by Holland? When by Denmark? Sweden? Spain? Russia?. 100

The Development of the Union

Who was the first president of the United States? In what
year was he elected? How long did he serve?........101, 144-145
Give a brief account of the life of George Washington........... 498
To what political party did Washington belong? State the
number of candidates for president of the United States
in 1789..144-145, 618
On what date was Washington inaugurated? In what city?
How was the date of inauguration chosen?..............170, 794
Of how many departments did Washington's cabinet consist?
Name them. Give the names of the members of Washington's
cabinet in 1789.......................................636-638
Which member of Washington's cabinet planned the organiza-
tion of the United States bank? Tell something of his life.652, 442
Where did the first congress of the United States meet? When?.101, 794
Name three states admitted to the Union during Washington's
administration... 101
During whose administration as president was the United States
supreme court organized? The first census enumeration
ordered? The first tariff bill passed?..................... 101
Who laid the cornerstone of the United States capitol? When
was the capital removed from Philadelphia to Washington?. 101
By whom was the cotton-gin invented? State some facts
about the inventor..................................101, 501
Name two political parties existing in Washington's time, and
state their views.. 171
Name the second president of the United States. How was the
vice-president chosen?...............................101, 171
Explain the alien and sedition laws. With what country was
the United States having trouble at the time these laws
were passed?... 171
Was John Adams a popular president? Give reasons......... 171
What president was elected by the house of representatives in
1800? Why?... 171

Why was the twelfth amendment to the constitution adopted? What are its provisions?..............................171, 598

Under whose administration was the District of Columbia established?... 101

Give an account of the purchase of Louisiana, telling from what nation it was purchased, the price paid, and the date of the transaction.................................171, 101, 130

Name two explorers who traveled through Oregon and Washington, 1804-1806. By whom were fur traders sent to these territories?...140, 179

Give an account of Aaron Burr's conspiracy. What office did he hold under President Jefferson?.................171, 414, 101

Who built the Clermont? When did she make her first trip from New York to Albany? What was her rate of speed?.101, 435

Explain the embargo act and the conditions that led to it. When was it passed? When was it repealed?..................171, 101

Name two important events of Adams's administration. Of Jefferson's... 101

Against what country did the United States declare war in 1812? Review the causes of this war..................101, 171

Mention four naval engagements in 1812. Compare results of the battles on the land with those on the water..........101, 171

Describe fully the battle of Lake Erie. What fact did this battle establish?...................................126, 476

What were the results of the battles at Chippewa and Lundy's Lane?...171, 130

Mention some buildings in Washington burned during the war of 1812. Give the date and some details of the attack.... 171

Name the treaty of peace closing the war of 1812. What battle took place after this treaty was signed?.................171, 164

Who commanded the American forces at the battle of New Orleans? Compare the two armies................102, 449, 171

Why was Monroe's administration called the "era of good feeling"?. 172

What were the provisions of the Missouri compromise? Why was it called a compromise?...........................172, 134

When and from what country did the United States acquire Florida?.......................................102, 110, 172

What are the principles of the Monroe doctrine? In what year was it proclaimed?...................................172, 102

Name the states admitted from 1803 to 1825, and state who was president when each was admitted..................101-102

Give briefly the most important facts in the lives of James Madison and James Monroe...........................461, 467

40

Mention five important events during the administration of James Madison. Of James Monroe....................101-102

In what year was the Erie canal completed? Where is it? State its length......................................102, 653

When was the first railroad built in the United States? What was its motive power? When was the first locomotive built in the United States?............................102, 674, 103

Mention a subject to which William Lloyd Garrison devoted much time after 1831. State the character of a book by William Ellery Channing published in 1841............436, 418

What position was taken by Andrew Jackson in regard to the United States bank?.................................... 172

State the origin of the political parties known as whigs and democrats..172, 171

Explain the nullification act of South Carolina. How was the affair finally settled?.................................. 172

Show why the attainments of the following entitle them to be regarded as noted Americans: Calhoun, Clay, Andrew Jackson, Daniel Webster......................................414-499

Relate the conditions existing in Texas early in the 19th century. Describe the battle of the Alamo...............160-161, 11, 103

Under whose administration was the Morse system of telegraphy patented? Between what cities was the first message sent?. 103

How long did William H. Harrison serve as president? By whom was he succeeded?................................ 103

What was the Dorr rebellion? State the causes...........42, 103

Name the official position held by Daniel Webster when the Ashburton treaty was signed. How did this treaty affect the state of Maine?.............................499, 103, 131

Give two important events from the administration of each of the following: John Quincy Adams, Andrew Jackson, Van Buren, Tyler...102-103

What was the Oregon question? Mention the two parallels named in the dispute. How was the matter settled?...... 172

State the cause of the war with Mexico in 1846. Name important battles and leaders. What territories did the United States acquire as a result of this war?..............172, 139, 103

Explain what is meant by the Wilmot proviso..............103, 173

Associate the name of each of the following with some crisis in American history: Sam Houston, Winfield Scott, Santa Ana, Zachary Taylor.................................447-493

Name the states admitted during the administrations of Jackson, Van Buren, Polk.......................................103, 624

Outline the principal events of James K. Polk's administration. 103, 477

What discovery greatly increased the population of California in 1849?..104, 33

Give full details of the compromise of 1850. Name its author. Which provision of this compromise is called the fugitive slave law?.. 173

How did the United States acquire New Mexico? What was the Gadsden purchase?................................ 135

What was the Kansas-Nebraska bill? When was it passed?...173, 104

Describe the feeling existing between the northern and southern states from 1850 to 1860. What was the principal issue?.. 173

Give facts about Stephen A. Douglas and Charles Sumner, showing their attitude towards the public questions of their time.428, 492

Explain the troubles in Kansas, 1854 to 1859...............173, 126

From what earlier political parties was the republican party of 1856 formed?... 173

Name the states admitted and other important events occurring during the administrations of Taylor, Fillmore, Pierce..... 104

During what years was James Buchanan president?............ 104

For what is Cyrus W. Field noted? When was the first message received over the Atlantic cable?......................433, 104

Which was the first southern state to secede from the Union?.... 104

Give the names of three men who were candidates for president of the United States in 1860. Which was elected?.619, 173, 104

Name the states which seceded from the Union in 1861........ 104

Where and when did the organization of the "Confederate States of America" take place? Who was chosen president?....104, 174

Give an account of the life of Jefferson Davis.................. 425

Describe the first attack on Fort Sumter. Who commanded the confederate forces? The union?....................174, 158

Give the date of the first battle of Bull Run. The second. In what state were these battles fought? Name the commanders. State the result............................32, 12

Name six battles of 1862—two fought in the North and four in the South... 105

By whom was New Orleans captured in 1862? Give facts about Farragut.......................................16, 105, 432

What was the nature of the emancipation proclamation? When and by whom was it issued?....................44-45, 105, 176

Name four important battles of 1863. Which army was victorious at Chancellorsville? At Chickamauga? At Gettysburg?.105, 11-19

Describe the battle of Gettysburg. Who were the commanders? Give its date... 115

Mention three battles of 1864. Which army was victorious in each?..105, 11-19

In what year was the battle of Antietam fought? The Wilderness? How many were killed and wounded in each battle?.11, 19

By what battle was the civil war terminated?................. 175

Review briefly the civil war, giving dates, battles, leaders, and result.. 139

Give facts about Robert E. Lee, stating his education and the wars in which he fought.............................. 456

When was General Lee made commander-in-chief of the confederate armies? Name four battles of the civil war in which he commanded................................... 456

What service did the following render the confederacy: Beauregard? Early? "Stonewall" Jackson? Albert Sidney Johnston? Joseph E. Johnston?...........................404-451

Give an account of the life of Ulysses S. Grant. In what year did he become commander-in-chief of the federal armies? When general of the army of the United States?........... 439

How did each of the following distinguish himself during the civil war: McClellan? Meade? Sheridan? Sherman?.........464-488

When was Abraham Lincoln assassinated? Sketch the principal events of his life. How long was he president?.......457, 144-145

By whom was Lincoln succeeded as president?................ 105

What two amendments to the constitution of the United States were proclaimed during Johnson's administration? State the purpose of each...........................105-106, 598-599

Tell fully how and when Alaska came into the possession of the United States....................................105, 177, 508

What conditions led to the impeachment of Andrew Johnson? Before what body was he tried? What was the verdict?..177, 451

Who became president of the United States in 1869?.........106, 439

What was the fifteenth amendment to the constitution? When was it ratified?..................................106, 598-599

For what claims was the Geneva award paid? State the amount. By what treaty was the matter adjusted?...........177, 106, 165

Give the history of the Alabama claims. How were they arbitrated? Who named the arbitrators?..................... 11

For what is Horace Greeley noted? When was he a candidate for president of the United States?....................440, 177

Who was Sitting Bull? How was he regarded by his tribe? What was his attitude toward the whites? What American general was killed in the battle of the Little Big Horn? Give date..106, 488

Name six notable events of Grant's administration............ 106

By what body was the election of president decided in 1876?
Which candidate was declared elected?..................... 177

Mention three events of Hayes's administration............... 106

How long did James A. Garfield serve as president? Give some
of his personal characteristics.................106, 144-145, 436

Who succeeded to the presidency after the assassination of
Garfield?... 106

Describe Bartholdi's statue of Liberty. Where is it? By whom
was it unveiled?....................................539, 107

Under whose administration was Chinese immigration prohibited?. 107

During whose administration was the McKinley tariff bill passed?
The Wilson tariff bill?..............................107, 108

Give the more important events of Cleveland's two administrations. Outline the leading facts of his life.....107-108, 420

What states were admitted under President Harrison?........ 107

In what year did McKinley take office as president?.......... 108

Name a tariff bill which became effective during McKinley's
administration... 108

What was the cause of the Spanish-American war?.........156, 38-39

Name the leading battles and the chief leaders of the Spanish-
American war. How long did this war last? How much
money did it cost the United States?.............139, 156-158

Describe the battle of Manila Bay. Name the American commander. Compare this battle with Trafalgar..........131, 427

Give facts about Sampson, Schley, and Roosevelt in connection
with the Spanish-American war...............156-157, 486, 482

For what military service is each of the following distinguished:
Adna R. Chaffee, Robley D. Evans, Richmond P. Hobson,
Nelson A. Miles, Charles D. Sigsbee, Joseph Wheeler,
Leonard Wood?......................................417-503

By what treaty was the Spanish-American war closed? What
territory did the United States acquire? How much money
did the United States pay to Spain?...............177, 164, 139

When did congress authorize self-government for Cuba? In
what year was the government formally transferred to the
Cuban authorities?................................... 39

When and in what city was President McKinley assassinated?
Sketch briefly the life of McKinley.................108, 177, 464

By whom was McKinley succeeded as president?.............. 108

Under whose administration was the Panama canal purchase
made? When was the treaty signed? What are its terms?.108, 553

What cabinet department was created in 1903?.............108, 639

In what year was Japanese immigration restrained?............ 177

When did the pure food law take effect?...................... 109

When was the San Francisco earthquake?..................... 109

Mention the leading events of Roosevelt's first administration. His second. Give a brief sketch of his life........108-109, 482

Name some prominent positions held by William H. Taft before his election to the presidency. When did he become president?... 492

What were the chief features of the Taft administration?...109, 178

Under whose administration was each of the following states admitted: Arizona? New Mexico? Oklahoma?.......... 109

When and by whom was the north pole discovered?......... 109

In what year were postal savings banks established? The parcel post system?............................109, 849, 848

When was the progressive party organized?.................. 94

When were the sixteenth and seventeenth amendments to the constitution ratified? In whose administrations? What are the provisions of these amendments?................109, 599

In what field of activity was Woodrow Wilson prominent before he entered political life? Give a brief sketch of his career..502-503

What are the noteworthy events of Wilson's administration?..109, 178

Who was president during the war of 1812? The war with Mexico in 1846? The civil war? The Spanish-American war? The world war?...........................139, 101-109

How many presidents served two full terms?................144-145

Which president served the shortest term?...................144-145

How many presidents were college men? How many were self-taught or had only common school education?.......144-145

How many presidents were born in the state in which you live?.144-145

Which state has produced the greatest number of presidents?.144-145

State the number of democratic presidents since 1860. Republican..144-145

Where is Lincoln buried? Grant? Fillmore?...............144-145

Which president once killed a man in a duel?................785-786

Mention a cabinet department created in 1913.................. 640

Associate each of the following names with some public enterprise: Jane Addams, Clara Barton, Andrew Carnegie, George W. Goethals, Jacob Riis.............................394-481

With what country and in what year was Perry's treaty made? How many important treaties in American history have been made at Paris?....................................... 164

Who is now president of the United States?.............144-145, 605

By whom was the gulf of St. Lawrence first explored? When?... 34

When and by whom was Quebec founded? What was the character of the settlement?......................34, 98, 562

State the year in which the French Jesuits settled at Port Royal. 98

Where was Fort St. Louis built? By whom?................. 34

Give an account of the life of Samuel de Champlain. When did he become governor of Canada?......................418, 98

What name was given to Canada by the French settlers?........ 805

By what people was Port Royal taken in 1628?............... 98

What country took Quebec in 1629? Name the leader........562, 98

How long after 1629 did the English hold Quebec? By whose influence was Canadian territory restored to the French? Give date...562, 98

Mention two classes of missionaries active in Canada early in the 17th century. Give three facts about them........ 34

By whom and when was Montreal founded? Who named the place?..546, 830

Name the first bishop of Quebec............................ 99

Mention a mission founded in 1668......................... 99

When was the Hudson bay company chartered? What territory was granted the company?............................... 34

From what stronghold and throughout what district did the French rule during the 17th century and the early half of the 18th century?...................................... 34

In what year did Frontenac become governor of Canada? Locate a fort named for him.............................. 99

Of the Indian tribes in Canada name one friendly to the English and one hostile tribe..................................... 34

What tribe of Indians captured Lachine?................... 99

During the greater part of the 18th century what European countries were struggling for control of America?......... 34

Name the principal event of King George's war..............168, 99

Name the leaders at the battle of Quebec. Which was victorious? On what "plains" was the battle fought? What contest was practically ended by this battle?.....34, 503, 467, 562

Give the date of the conquest of Montreal by the English. State the importance of this capitulation....................34, 546

By what treaty of peace was the French and Indian war ended? What were its terms?................................168, 34

How were Montreal and Quebec affected by the American revolution?...546, 100

At what time were St. John, N. B., and Kingston, Ontario, founded?.. 100

In what year was Canada divided into Upper and Lower Canada? What was the character of each division?.................101, 34

When and by whom was the city of Toronto founded? Give the name of the fort which formerly occupied the site of Toronto..575, 99, 844

At what time was slavery rendered illegal in Upper Canada? In Lower Canada? Was this earlier or later than the abolition of slavery throughout the British dominions?............101, 155

Who was the founder of Ottawa? By what name was Ottawa formerly known?..................................... 551

In what year was the Welland canal completed? What cities does it connect?... 102

When was constitutional government granted to Newfoundland? 103

At what time were Upper and Lower Canada reunited for legislative purposes?.. 34

What city became the capital of Canada in 1858?.............. 104

By what legislative act were the British colonies in North America united? What name was given to their union?.............34,53

Name the colonies included in the Dominion of Canada at the time it was constituted. Mention three others added from 1868 to 1873. What colony refused to join the confederacy?..34, 105, 106

Who was the first governor-general of Canada?................ 151

Name the first premier of Canada. Mention other important offices held by him What was his influence in the federation of the colonies?................................152, 460

Give a brief sketch of the life of Alexander Mackenzie. What honor did he decline?.................................... 460

What agitation took place in Nova Scotia in 1868?............ 106

State the cause of Riel's rebellion. How was it suppressed? Give its date..................................... 34

In what circumstances was Manitoba organized? What name was given to the unorganized territory beyond Manitoba?... 34

Name the divisions of the Northwest Territory made in 1882.... 107

By what treaty of 1871 was the fisheries dispute with the United States settled? What arrangement was made?............ 34

Describe the second rebellion headed by Louis Riel.............34-35

When did the Washington treaty expire? How did its expiration affect the fisheries question?........................ 35

How and when was the Bering sea question settled?............ 35

In what year was the controversy over the Alaskan boundary decided? In favor of which country?...................35, 108

When was the Canadian Pacific railway completed?............ 107

In what year was the Canadian-Australian cable laid?.......... 108

When was the university of Ottawa founded? McGill university? King's College, Windsor, N. S.?......................100-108

In what year did the first transatlantic steamer arrive at Quebec? When was the suspension bridge at Niagara Falls opened? The Grand Trunk railroad?............................. 104

At what time did Canada adopt the decimal system of coinage?.. 104

What administration changes occurred in 1911? What reciprocal measure was defeated at the same time?.................109, 35

State the important facts from the lives of Sir Charles Tupper, Sir Wilfrid Laurier, Robert Laird Borden, Duke of Connaught, Baron Strathcona, Sir Lomer Gouin............409-495

Name the present governor-general of Canada. The present premier..151, 152

MEXICO

According to traditional history what different dates are given for the occupation of Mexico by the Toltecs?.....98, 132, 162

Describe the Toltecs—their mode of life, their religion, their progress and civilization.........................132, 162-163

What was the fate of the Toltecs in Mexico? By whom were they succeeded? Give the approximate date........132, 162, 98

Give an account of the government of the Aztecs. Of their religion... 132

When was the city of Mexico founded? What is the origin of its name?......................................98, 132, 829

Name the first Spanish discoverer to visit Mexico. Give the date. What sort of government did he set up?....132, 423, 98

With what territories was Mexico united in 1540? Under what name? How was all this territory governed?........... 132

How did Mexico rank with other Spanish colonies? With what country was Mexico compelled to carry on all its foreign trade?...132-133

For how long did Spain rule Mexico? Under what circumstances was the republic of Mexico established?.................132-133

Who became president of Mexico in 1833? Give the leading events of his life....................................103, 485

Give the dates connected with the independence of Texas. What war was the result of the annexation of Texas by the United States?...133, 103

Name the Mexican leader in the war against the United States
    in 1846. State the result of the war...................... 139
Sketch affairs in Mexico from 1855 to 1867.................... **133**
By what country was the Emperor Maximilian sent to Mexico?.. **133**
How long did Maximilian rule Mexico? How did the empire
    end? Who resumed the government of Mexico?........**105, 133**
In what year did Porfirio Diaz become president of Mexico?
    How long did he serve? Name two events of his admin-
    istration......................................**133, 427, 109**
Why did Porfirio Diaz resign as president? Give facts about
    Madero...**133, 109**
Who led an insurrection beginning in 1912?................. **133**
Name the leader of an insurrection commencing in 1913........ **109**
What led the U. S. to take Vera Cruz in 1914?............... **133**

SOUTH AMERICA

When did the Incas rule Peru?.............................. 120
By whom was Peru conquered in 1533?.................**120, 477**
Who were the first two European explorers of Argentina? At
    what time were their explorations made?.................. 20
When was Buenos Ayres founded? Why was the site chosen?
    What does its name mean?..........................**20, 804**
From what European country did some of the colonists of
    Argentina come?..................................... 20
Where did the Spanish establish themselves in 1729?.......... 99
Until 1775, how was Argentina governed? What change of
    government was made in that year? What territory was
    added? What city became the capital?...............**20, 100**
What people regarded Titicaca as a sacred place? Tell one of
    their legends... 844
When were Buenos Ayres and Montevideo occupied by the
    English? What was the effect on the colonists?......... 20
In what year did the independence of Argentina begin?.......**101, 20**
What confederation was formed in 1816? In 1831? Describe
    conditions in the Argentine confederation, 1831 to 1859... 20
When was the constitution of Argentina decreed?.............. 102
Mention the territories acquired by Argentina in 1881. Between
    what two countries were Patagonia and Tierra del Fuego
    divided?..**20, 106**
Tell something of the development of railroads in Argentina..**108, 20**
How did Argentina restrict immigration in 1911?............ 20

Name a large battleship launched for the Argentine navy. Give date... 109

Make a statement about Argentina's expenditures for education in recent years.. 20

Name the president of Argentina..........................604-605

What Portuguese navigator discovered Brazil? When?....... 143

When did Amerigo Vespucci visit Brazil?.................... 396

Who made the first settlement in Brazil? In what year?...... 31

Under the power of what country did Brazil fall in 1578? To what country did it become a prey?...................... 31

When did Portugal recover Brazil from the Hollanders?.......31, 84

Why was the seat of Portuguese government once at Rio de Janeiro? When did Brazil become a kingdom?.......143, 31, 102

Who was the "perpetual defender" of Brazil? When did he proclaim the independence of the country?............31-32, 102

When was the republic of Brazil founded?.................... 32

What important international steps were taken by Brazil during the year 1906?... 32

Name a conference held at Rio de Janeiro in 1906........... 109

What demonstration of international interest was given by Rio de Janeiro in 1908?.. 32

Who is the president of Brazil?..........................604-605

To whom did Chile originally belong? By whom was it conquered in 1535?... 35

When and by whom was Santiago founded?.................... 839

For how many years was Chile a Spanish colony? When did Chile gain her independence?............................. 35

Compare Chile with other South American states with respect to internal disturbances.................................. 35

From what countries did Chile gain large territories in 1881?..35, 106

What serious disaster visited Valparaiso in 1906? 788

Who is now president of Chile?..........................604-605

Give facts about Atahualpa, Simon Bolivar, Santos-Dumont.. 400-485

HISTORY OF CONTINENTAL EUROPE

ITALY

Under whom did the kingdom of Italy begin? By what conqueror of Italy was he put to death?..................66, 67

Who was Belisarius? Justinian? For whom did Belisarius take Italy?...................................405, 452, 67

What parts of Italy did the Lombards conquer? Give date. Give meaning of the name Lombards...................127, 67

Where and when was Charlemagne crowned king of Italy? What other countries did he rule?.........................69, 418

To what empire did southern Italy become subject in 890 A. D.?. 70

Where, when, and by whom was Otto I crowned king of Italy? Of what country was he already king?..................... 473

In what year was Italy united to Germany?................... 73

What is meant by the two Sicilies?......................... 154

By whom was Sicily taken from the Saracens? What title did his son receive?......................................75, 482

In what century did Venice become a great maritime power? From what period does the cathedral of St. Mark date?...75, 576

Who were the Ghibellines? The Guelphs? What influence had their feud upon Italy?............................ 115

What were the Sicilian vespers?..........................123, 155

State some facts about Savonarola. When did he live?...... 485

Describe the progress made by the republics of Italy during the 12th and 13th centuries. How did these conditions lead to the downfall of the states?...................... 123

When did the dominion of Italy pass to the pope?............. 76

Give an account of Dante's life. Why was he banished?...... 424

Who was Lorenzo de' Medici? For what was the Medici family distinguished?...465, 80

For what is the pontificate of Pope Leo X noted? How was he related to Lorenzo de' Medici?...................80, 456, 26

For what is Michaelangelo famed? Of what great structure was he the architect?...........................397-398, 572

Give the date of Napoleon's Italian campaign................ 86

When was the Italian republic proclaimed? Who became its president?..86, 88

What coronation took place at Milan in 1805? How long did the kingdom of Italy last?........................543-544, 88

After the fall of Napoleon by what authority was Italy reconstituted?... 123

What was the result of the revolution of 1848? Explain what Cavour accomplished for Italy at this time..............91, 417

When did Victor Emmanuel become king of Sardinia, and when king of Italy?..497, 93

Describe Garibaldi's career. Mention one of his conquests....436, 123

When did Rome become the capital of Italy? Under what control was Rome from 728 to 1870?....................95, 567

What is the vatican? Under whose power is it?............576, 567

With whom was Italy at war, 1911-12? State result.........123, 139

Sketch briefly facts about the following: Raphael, Titian, Leonardo da Vinci....................................479-497

What did Galileo do toward the progress of science? What opposition did he meet?................................. 435

What Italian city was the birthplace of Christopher Columbus? What great discovery did he make? Give date.......421, 98

THE EASTERN EMPIRE
TURKEY, OR THE OTTOMAN EMPIRE

When did Justinian become emperor of the east? What were the characteristics of his reign?........................67, 452

Mention some territory acquired by the eastern empire before 600 A. D. Give the extent of the empire in 600...........67, 68

How was Constantinople twice saved from the Saracens?...... 68

From what part of the world did the Ottoman Turks come?... 166

When were the Turks first recognized as a nation?............ 67

From whom did the Turks get their religion? In what century?. 166

What does Ottoman mean? Who was Othman?............833, 166

By whom was the Ottoman empire founded? When?.......... 76

When did the Ottomans establish themselves in Europe?....... 79

Trace the Ottoman encroachments upon the eastern empire......78-80

For what purpose did John VII of the eastern empire visit Italy?. 78

When did the eastern empire end? How long had it existed?..80, 42

During the 14th and 15th centuries what was the military rank of the Turkish empire?............................... 166

Mention the territory acquired by Turkey between 1360 and 1520...166, 81-83

By whom was the Turkish navy created? In what century?.. 166

Under whom did the Ottoman empire reach its greatest power?.. 166

For what was Solyman the Magnificent celebrated?.........166, 489

Mention the first great naval defeat and the first great reverse on land which the Ottoman empire met................... 166

When was the battle of Lepanto fought? By whom?.......166, 127
Name Turkey's strongest opponent in the 18th century......... 166
What Russian territory did Turkey hold at the middle of the
    18th century?.. 166
When did the Turkish empire lose the Crimea?..............167, 87
By what means and at what time did Greece become independent
    of Turkey?... 167
Give the cause of the Crimean war. What countries united with
    Turkey in that war?................................167, 38
What was the result of the Crimean war?...................167, 139
Explain the causes and the results of the Russo-Turkish war.167, 139
Name the territory lost by Turkey between 1878 and 1885.... 167
By whom was Abdul-Hamid forced to abdicate? What is the
    order of succession to the Turkish throne?.............167, 393
Give the cause and the result of the Balkan war............167, 139

SPAIN AND PORTUGAL

By what names was Spain known to the Greeks and to the
    Romans? Why was Spain so named?..................155, 842
In what century and by whom was Barcelona founded and
    named?...155-156, 801
In what order was Spain successively controlled by the Moors,
    the Visigoths, the Greeks, the Romans? Trace the same
    nations in Portugal................................156, 142
Under the power of what invading nation was Spain at the time
    of the fall of the western empire, 476 A. D.? What invaders
    made Toledo their capital?............................156, 844
Describe conditions in Spain under Roman rule............... 156
When did the Moors obtain control of Spain? When did they
    lose it? When were the last Moors expelled?.........156, 19, 82
In what century did small Christian kingdoms begin to spring
    up in Moorish Spain?................................. 156
What is the Alhambra? When was it founded?..............798, 77
Show how Ferdinand V of Castile became monarch of all the
    Spanish kingdoms.....................................432, 156
When was the conquest of Granada made?..................80, 156
Name an important discovery made during the reign of Ferdi-
    nand and Isabella. Give the date.....................432-433
What Portuguese city was the market of the world in the 16th
    century?....... 82
Mention some celebrated Portuguese navigators, their voyages
    and discoveries....................................... 143
When did Spain acquire the Philippines?..................... 82

Between what dates was Portugal under Spanish rule?........82, 84

Describe the Spanish armada. In what year and with what object
was it sent out? What was the result?................... 21

Under what ruler were Mexico and Peru added to Spain? Give
dates..156, 83

When did the war of the Spanish succession occur? Give result.156, 139

Why did Spain declare war against Napoleon in 1808? What
country aided Spain in this war, and with what result?..... 156

When was Portugal released from Napoleon's power? When did
it become a constitutional monarchy? A republic?........ 143

Upon the abdication of what ruler did Spain become a republic?
How soon was the monarchy restored?................... 156

State the cause of the Spanish-American war. What possessions
did Spain lose as a result of this war?..................156, 139

Who were Cervantes, Cid, Cortez, Velasquez, Magellan?.....417-496

FRANCE

By what name was France known to the Romans? What
Roman ruler first conquered France?....................110, 63

Give the origin of the name France. When are the Franks
first mentioned in history?............................815, 65

How early was Paris known to the Romans? When and under
whom did the Franks take Paris?......................555, 66

Under what power was Gaul when the western empire fell?...66, 110

Who was the founder of the French monarchy?...........67, 421, 110

To what dynasty did Clovis I belong? How long did the Mero-
vingians rule France?................................110, 147

What was the Salic law?..............................153-154, 67

Who was Charles Martel? What decisive battle in the world's
history did he win?...................................419, 22

Name the founder of the Carlovingian dynasty.............147, 476

During whose rule did France reach its greatest power?........110, 418

Between what years was Charlemagne king of France?.......... 147

Who was the founder of the new western empire? In what year?
Over what countries did he rule?.......................69, 418

Explain the song of Roland and its connection with French
history..382, 378

Trace the divisions of the empire among the descendants of
Charlemagne.. 69

How and when did Normandy get its name? Who were the
Northmen?..136, 832

Name the first king of the house of Capet. Over what European countries has the house of Capet ruled?............148, 415

At what time was the French language first written?.......72, 293

What were the crusades? Name three French rulers who led the crusades.......................................38, 75, 77

When was the university of Paris founded? What colleges existed in Paris prior to that time?......................76, 111

Which king first levied a tax to maintain a standing army?..... 111

By virtue of what law did Philippe of Valois become king?...... 111

Between whom and when did the hundred years' war occur? Name king of France at the beginning and at the close....138, 148

What country was victorious in each of the following battles: Crécy, Poitiers, Agincourt?.........................527, 78, 111

What part did Joan of Arc play in bringing the hundred years' war to a close? What title is applied to her?......399, 111, 81

What was the Bastille?...................................... 518

Who were the troubadours? Name the first troubadour of note..385, 74

Sketch the conditions which brought about the *renaissance*...... 294

Who were the Huguenots? Under what French king did their persecution begin?.................................,...118, 111

Describe the massacre of St. Bartholomew. Who instigated it?...118, 153, 111, 417

Who was the first king of the house of Bourbon?.............148, 111

By what edict were the rights of the Huguenots established? What war did this close?.....................118, 42, 164, 138

When did Cardinal Richelieu administer the government?.....111, 480

Give an account of the reign of Louis XIV. What cardinal was his prime minister?................................459, 464

From what is the name Fronde derived? When did the wars of the Fronde occur?.................................... 113

By whom was the edict of Nantes revoked?...................42, 85

How did the American war for independence influence the people of France during the latter part of the 18th century?. 111

State the conditions which led to the French revolution begun in the reign of Louis XVI. How long did it last?........459, 139

Sketch briefly the life of Marie Antoinette..................... 398

What class of people composed the *tiers état?* What other classes controlled most of the wealth of France?.................. 162

What is meant by the states general?...........................842

When did the national assembly begin? By what other name was it known? What did it do?.............................. 21

What was the national guard? When organized? Give facts about its first commander.........................113, 87, 455

What action was taken by the legislative assembly?............ 21

When did the "convention" meet? What did it proclaim?...... 21

Who were the Girondists? When did most of them perish?..115-116

Who were the Jacobins? What political power did they exert?.123-124

What organization was responsible for the reign of terror? When
did it begin?.......................................124, 113

Give facts from the life of Danton, Marat, Robespierre, Charlotte Corday, Madame Roland........................422-482

Mention the principal events of the French revolution......112-113

What was the French directory? Of how many members was
it composed?.. 41

Who became commander of the French army in 1795?.......... 87

When was the directory overthrown? By whom? What official
position did he take? How long did the consulate last?. 112, 469, 148

What is the legion of honor? Who instituted it?...........366, 793

When was Napoleon I proclaimed emperor of France? How long
did he reign? Explain the cause of his downfall....89, 148, 470

After the abdication of Napoleon, to what island was he exiled?
How long did he remain there in exile?..............469-470, 813

Sketch briefly the life of Napoleon I.......................469-470

Upon the restoration of the Bourbon line who became king?.148, 112

What was the hundred days' war? What battle ended it?....470, 112

Describe the battle of Waterloo. Name the leaders. Give
the result. Why is this battle of particular importance?.179, 22

To what island was Napoleon I banished after his defeat at
Waterloo? When did he die?........................... 112

For what purpose was the holy alliance formed? What countries entered into it?..........................89, 117-118, 164

Name the leading battles and chief leaders of the Napoleonic
wars. What position did France hold at their close?...... 139

How was the reign of Charles X affected by the revolution of
1830?...112, 148

When did the second republic begin? Who was its president?
Under what title did he become emperor?........148, 112, 470

In what war was the battle of Sedan fought? What emperor
was captured? Give facts about the battle.............139, 112

Give the chief facts in the history of Alsace-Lorraine......... 11

What change of government followed the defeat and the capture
of Napoleon III?...................................... 148

What were the Tuileries?................................... 165

In what wars did Bazaine and MacMahon distinguish themselves? Which commanded at Sedan? Which at Metz?.404, 460

Mention five kings of France who were deposed............. 41

When did the final disposition of the Dreyfus case occur?....... 112

For how many years has France been a republic?.............. 148

To whom was the Nobel prize for chemistry awarded in 1911?.. 97

Connect each of the following with some important period in
French history: Condé, Grouchy, Turenne..............421-495

For what is each of the following celebrated: Bonheur? Doré?
Eiffel? Rodin?.......................................409-481

Who is the present president of France?.....................605

GERMANY

What is the meaning of the name Germany?.................. 816

Who were the Teutones? What region is supposed to have
been their original settlement?........................... 160

When did the Teutones invade Gaul? Compare with the date
of the first great migration of the German nations.......160, 62

By whom were the Germans defeated in 55 B. C.?............. 63

Where did the Frisians live? When and by whom were they
subjected to Roman rule?.............................. 113

Name two German cities which grew out of the fixed camps of
the Roman legions.................................... 64

Give the year in which Germanicus subdued Germany......... 64

In what manner did Varus govern lower Germany? Who was
emperor of Rome at that time?.........................64, 146

When was a Roman bridge built across the Danube? Under
what Roman emperor? 65, 146

Mention a wall built in Germany by the Roman emperor Hadrian. 65

Where did the Goths originally dwell? Name the two divisions
into which they separated in the 3rd century. Where did
each division settle?................................... 116

What people established a confederacy in Germany at the middle
of the 3rd century?................................... 65

From what people did Hungary take its name? What was its
ancient name?.......................................821, 65

When did the Huns invade Hungary? Where did they come
from? Why are the Germans called Huns?..........821, 119, 65

When did Teutonic tribes first overrun Alsace-Lorraine?........ 11

Where did the Lombards live? In what century did they leave
their original location? How far south did they migrate?. 127

In what parts of Germany did France claim supremacy? Where
did the Franks set up their kingdom?...................66, 113

Who are the Czechs? When did they settle in Bohemia?.... 528

When did Charlemagne become king of Germany, Italy, and
France? What was the character of his reign?.......69, 418, 113

What king is regarded as the founder of the German empire?
How was he related to Charlemagne?...................149, 69

When did the Carlovingian dynasty end? At this period what nations were in Germany? By whom was their king crowned?...149, 113-114

Mention some conquests made during the reigns of Henry the Fowler and Otho the Great........................149, 114, 473

During the 10th century what was the attitude of the Hungarians towards other nations? Who subdued them? When did Hungary become subject to Germany?........118, 114

Give the main facts of the disagreement between Henry IV of Germany and Pope Gregory VII................75, 445, 440, 522

When did the Hohenstauffen dynasty begin?................... 149

Under whose reign did the wars of the Guelphs and the Ghibellines begin? At what time? Explain their strife....114, 149, 115

When was the Hanseatic league formed? Explain why the Hanse towns formed a league..........................77, 117

By what emperor was the house of Habsburg founded? What historic feud did he terminate?....................114, 149, 483

What invention was made by Gutenberg? Where? When?...441, 80

Of what country is it said that its history is the history of the house of Habsburg?..................................... 22

In what century and under what Austrian ruler was Hungary united to Austria?..22, 118

When did the reformation begin? In whose reign?.....80, 150, 464

Give a brief sketch of the life of Martin Luther............ 460

What was the attitude of Charles V towards the reformation? State the importance of the period in which he reigned... 418

When was the diet of Worms held? What was it? What plea did Luther make?................................82, 165, 460

Of what did the confession of Augsburg consist? What was its purpose? Give facts about the compiler................688, 465

Explain the cause of the thirty years' war. Give the dates, the leading battles, the chief leaders..................114, 161, 138

What was the defenestration of Prague?....................39, 560

Name the countries involved in the thirty years' war. By what treaty was it closed?..............................161-162, 114

Give facts about Tilly. Wallenstein......................495, 497

By what country was Maria Theresa supported in her contest for the throne of Germany? How long did the war of the Austrian succession last?...............................462, 139

When and where was the battle of Lützen fought? In what war? What king was killed in this battle?............131, 441

In what condition did the thirty years' war leave Germany?... 114

Name the chief contestants in the seven years' war. What
    nations were involved? State its effect upon Prussia...154, 51, 139
Give some facts from the life of Frederick the Great of Prussia... 434
When did Francis II of Germany take the title of Emperor of
    Austria? By whom was he driven out of Germany?....88, 22
At what time was Germany under the power of Napoleon? How
    was it governed during that period?.................114, 150, 37
State the object of the holy alliance. When was it formed?...117-118
How long did the Germanic confederation rule? By what vote
    was Austria excluded from the confederation?.......150, 114
State the cause of the seven weeks' war. Name the principal
    battles. How did it result?............................114, 139
In what year was Austria finally excluded from Germany?
    What is meant by the North German confederation? How
    long did it rule Germany?..........................22, 136, 150
Who became king of Prussia in 1861? Premier in 1862?........ 92
When was the Franco-Prussian war? Name the leading battles.
    The chief leaders. What did Germany gain by this war?.139, 114
Give the effects of German rule in Alsace-Lorraine............. 11
Tell some facts about Bismarck, Frederick Charles, von Moltke.
    Which commanded the German forces at Gravelotte?
    Which received a title in recognition of his services during
    the Franco-Prussian war?............................407-467
When was the Germanic empire reconstructed? Who was its
    first emperor? How long had he been king of Prussia?.114, 150, 502
In what year did William II become emperor of Germany? What
    characteristics make his reign conspicuous?.........150, 502, 114
Name the present ruler of Germany.......................... 605

AUSTRIA-HUNGARY

By what battle of the seven weeks' war was Austria perma-
    nently separated from Germany? Give date.............22, 119
In what respects is the government of Hungary distinct from
    that of Austria?......................................22, 119
When did Austria pass a universal suffrage law?............... 94
What territories were acquired by Austria in 1909?............ 22
When did Francis Joseph become emperor of Austria? When
    was he crowned king of Hungary? Outline the principal
    events of his reign..................................434, 119
For what was Metternich distinguished? Kossuth?..........466, 454
Who is now ruler of Austria-Hungary?...................... 605

DENMARK

Give the meaning of the name Scandinavia. In early literature
what people were called Scandinavians?...............840, 286

How early did the Romans know the inhabitants of Denmark?..   40

Who was Odin? Name the mythical first ruler of Denmark....40, 337

Name two classes into which the early people of Denmark were
divided, and state their occupations......................   40

Give the date of the first recorded invasion of Britain by the
Danes, or Northmen...................................69, 136

Who was the first authentic king of Denmark? What countries
did he unite? In what country did his descendants reign?.40, 71

What are the Eddas? When were they composed? What is
meant by the sagas?...........................286, 354, 379

When did Canute reign in England? When did his dynasty in
Denmark end?...................................415, 150, 40

State the extent of the Danish kingdom in the 12th and 13th
centuries...   40

Mention a queen who ruled Norway, Sweden, and Denmark. By
what act were these countries united?..............40, 462, 164

When was the union of Calmar dissolved?.....................   83

How long did the Oldenburg line rule Denmark?...............   40

Who was the ablest Danish ruler? When did he reign?........40, 83

At what time was serfdom prevalent in Denmark? What king
was active in abolishing serfdom?........................   40

What effect have the Schleswig-Holstein troubles produced?.....   40

Who is the present king of Denmark?........................   605

When, to what country, and for what sum did Denmark sell the
Virgin islands?...................................41, 577, 624

SWEDEN AND NORWAY

Divide the early inhabitants of Sweden into two groups. State
their origin. How did an attempt to unite them result?....   158

From what deity did the Ynglingar dynasty claim descent?..158, 337

Who were Odin, Frigga, Thor?...........................330-342

Give the origin of Friday, Thursday, Wednesday............816-846

Name a king who ruled the whole of Sweden. When?.........   158

When and by whom was Stockholm founded? What does its
name mean?.......................................571, 842

Who was the first Christian king of Sweden?.................   73

Who became king of Sweden in 1150? Why did his death cause
trouble with Denmark?............................75, 158

When was the throne of Sweden offered to the ruler of another
country?...159, 462

What countries were united by the union of Calmar? Give
date..159, 164, **462**

When were the Danes driven from Sweden? Who then became
king of Sweden?................................159, 83, **441**

In what condition did Gustaf Vasa leave Sweden at his death?.. **159**

How did Sweden become involved in the thirty years' war?
Who was king of Sweden? Where was he killed?....161-162, **131**

How does Gustavus Adolphus rank with other rulers of his time?
When did he reign?.................................159, **441**

When was Sweden declared an absolute monarchy?............ **85**

Characterize the reign of Charles XII of Sweden..........418, 85, **87**

Who was Bernadotte? How did he become king of Sweden?
Characterize his reign and the Bernadotte dynasty.......406, **159**

In what year were Norway and Sweden united as two kingdoms
under one monarch? How long did this union continue? 89, 95, **159**

For what is each of the following noted: Alstroemer? Ericsson?
Linnæus? Oxenstierna? Swedenborg?...................396-**492**

Name the present king of Sweden........................... **605**

With the history of what countries is that of Norway interwoven?.. **137**

Who was the first king of Norway?......................... **71**

In what century does the authentic history of Norway begin?.... **137**

What expeditions led to the introduction of Christianity?..... **137**

When did Olaf II rule Norway? Name a king with whom Olaf
was at war. To what country did Norway pass as a result
of that war?.......................................137, **472**

In what year was Bergen built?............................. **75**

Explain the conditions that brought Norway under the rule of
Queen Margaret. What other countries did she rule?..137, **462**

When was Norway first united to Denmark? During what critical
period in European history was this union severed?........ **137**

Why was Denmark compelled to give up Norway? With what
country did the treaty of Kiel unite Norway?...........137, **164**

How did the Norwegians receive the treaty of Kiel? Why did
Bernadotte invade their country?....................... **137**

On what conditions did Norway consent to Swedish government?
Who was the first joint king of Sweden and Norway?...... **137**

What caused the final separation of Norway from Sweden?
When did it occur? Who became king of Norway?...137, 95, **159**

When was the first book printed in Norway? What was it?.... **289**

What great discovery was made by Roald Amundsen in 1911?
Sketch his career....................................94, **397**

Who were Björnson, Ole Bornemann Bull, Ibsen, Nansen?......407-**469**

Give the name of the present king of Norway................. **605**

RUSSIA

Who is regarded as the founder of Russia? State his nationality, the territory controlled by him, and the date of the founding of the empire.. 152

What Russian ruler invaded Constantinople in the 10th century? Name an invasion made by him in 907....................70-71

Who became ruler of Russia in 945?........................ 71

What ruler is called the Charlemagne of Russia? When did he reign? Mention some of his deeds......................152, 73

Describe conditions in Russia during the 11th and 12th centuries..152, 73

Name two Russian cities founded in the 12th century.......... 75

Give the approximate date of the Mongol invasion of Russia. By what name were the invaders known? Until what date was Russia under Tartar rule?..........................77, 79

Give the year in which Ivan the Great became ruler of Russia. What title did he assume?..........................81, 149

What was the character of the rule of Ivan the Terrible? When did he reign?.....................................315, 83, 149

By whom was the house of Romanoff founded?...............83, 149

State facts about the reign of Alexis........................149, 395

Give an account of the reign of Peter the Great. Why is it said that Russia's greatness dates from his accession?.....149, 152, 476

Who founded St. Petersburg? Give details............834, 85, 572

When and under what ruler did the three partitions of Poland take place? What portion of Poland did Russia receive?..164, 152, 142

Describe the reign of Catherine II..........................149, 417

In what battles was Russia engaged during the reign of Alexander I? What wars were then taking place throughout Europe? 395, 139

When was Poland united to Russia? When did it become a part of the Russian empire?......................89, 152, 142

Name a war which was terminated by Alexander II. By means of what treaty? What death did Alexander II meet?.395, 164, 152

Give a brief account of the Crimean war and its consequences. Name some of the battles..........................38, 152, 139

To whom and when was Russian America sold?................ 93

With what country was Russia at war in 1877?..............139, 152

What territory was acquired by Russia from 1858 to 1909?..... 152

In what year did Nicholas II come to the throne? State some of his personal characteristics. Mention important events during his reign....................................149, 471

What privileges were given by China to Russia in 1900? How did this lead to the Russo-Japanese war?................152-153

Name the leading battles and the chief leaders of the Russo-Japanese war. Give its result..........................139, 153
Give the origin of these names: Moscow, Russia, Warsaw......830-846
At about what time did the spread of nihilism begin? Who is Prince Kropotkin?...............................95, 152, 454
Give facts about Gorky, Kosciusko, Stolypin, Tolstoi, Witte...439-503
Give the chief facts concerning Russia's part in the world war...97, 153

BELGIUM AND HOLLAND

In the time of Cæsar what name was given to the territory now known as Belgium? What was its extent? How long did it continue under Roman rule?........................... 22
How early is Antwerp mentioned in history?.................. 510
Trace the history of Belgium from the fall of Rome to 953. Into what parts was Belgium divided in 953?...................22-23
What royal house acquired the whole of the Netherlands in the 15th century? For how many years had Holland been an independent country?..................................23, 117
When and why did Belgium and Holland become Austrian possessions? Why did they later pass under Spanish rule?......23, 117
When and under whom did the seven northern states establish their independence? What country retained Belgium?.....23, 117
Outline the changes made in the territory and government of Belgium from 1598 to 1714. What disposal was made of Belgium by the treaty of Utrecht? What name was given to Belgium by that treaty?.............................. 23
By whom was Belgium conquered during the Austrian war of succession? What restoration was made in 1748? By what treaty?... 23
At what time did the Belgians attempt to set up an independent government as United Belgium? Trace the happenings of the next ten years.................................... 23
When was the kingdom of the Netherlands formed? Of what countries was it composed? Who became king?.......23, 89, 117
How long did the kingdom of the Netherlands exist? Why was it dissolved? Who was made king of Belgium?........23, 89
What was the character of the reign of Leopold I of Belgium?.456, 23
How long did Leopold II rule Belgium?.....................456, 23
By what treaty was the Congo Free State constituted? Who became its sovereign? To what country was the Congo State annexed in 1908?................................ 23
For what are Rubens and Van Dyck celebrated?............483, 496

Who is now king of Belgium?............................. 605

Give the chief facts concerning the German invasion of Belgium
    in 1914... 23

How many provinces united to form the Union of Utrecht?
    By what collective name were these provinces known?...... 117

Give an account of the life of Hugo Grotius.................. 440

Who was John de Witt? What positions did he hold?.........85, 427

When were Holland and Belgium united? Give the name of
    the kingdom thus formed. Name the ruler............. 117

In what year did Holland become a separate kingdom? How long
    did William I continue to rule Holland?.................117, 91

How many years did William III reign in Holland?............ 117

Give a brief sketch of the life of Wilhelmina of Holland......... 501

What international court of arbitration meets at the Hague?
    When was it established?............................... 603

To what country is the name Netherlands now restricted?.... 548

Name the present ruler of the Netherlands................... 605

MODERN GREECE

When was Greece taken from the eastern empire by the Latins?.. 116

By whom and when was Greece added to the Turkish empire?
    How long did Greece remain a Turkish province?........166, 116

Give date and result of the war of Greek independence....116, 89, 139

When was the kingdom of Greece founded? Give nationality
    of the first king..................................89, 116

In what year did the people demand a constitution? When was
    the king forced to abdicate?...........................91, 117

Give the name and nationality of the second king of Greece..... 117

When did Greece annex the Ionian isles?....................93, 117

What was the result of the war with Turkey in 1896?.......... 117

With whom did Greece engage in war in 1912? What countries
    united with Greece?................................117, 167

What territory did Greece acquire in the Balkan war?........536, 117

Name the present king of Greece............................97, 605

HISTORY OF ASIATIC COUNTRIES

THE SARACENS

What Semitic chiefs are supposed to have been the fathers of the present inhabitants of Arabia?............................ 19

With what great religious character does the history of Arabia begin?.. 19

At what time did the Jews migrate into Arabia? What conditions were favorable to the introduction of Mohammedanism?..... 19

Sketch the life of Mohammed................................ 467

When was the Koran published? What does it contain? Explain the doctrines of Mohammedanism...................68, 282, 717

Who succeeded Mohammed? Give some facts about Abu Bekr..717, 393

During how many centuries does the dominion of the Arabs form an important period in the history of civilization?........19, 467

When did the Saracens take Jerusalem? How long did they hold it?... 68

In what century was the power of the caliphs established in the east? What authority had the caliphs? What does the word caliph mean?...................................68, 34

When was Mohammedanism accepted in Persia?............... 68

What part of Africa was subdued by the Saracens in 698? In 709?... 68

When was the art of paper-making introduced by the Arabs?.. 68

How large a portion of Spain was acquired by the Moors in 711? How did they govern it?................................ 156

Trace the attacks and conquests made by the Saracens from 673 to 1055..68-73

In what battle were the Saracens defeated by France? Of what importance was this battle?........................69, 22

When did Bagdad become the capital of the Saracenic empire? Under whom did it attain its greatest splendor?...........69, 34

Who was Haroun al Raschid? What famous romances date from his time?................................69, 443, 362

Whose reign was called the golden period of learning in Arabia? In what country did the Saracens promote agriculture and horticulture at this time?............................282, 69

By whom and when were the figures of arithmetic brought into Europe?... 70

When did the decline of the caliphate begin? In what year
was Bagdad overthrown by the Turks? When did the
caliphate of Bagdad come to an end?...................70, 73, 19
State the results of the Saracen conquests from 710 to 1492.
The leading battles. The chief leaders................... 138
When and by whom was the Alhambra founded? When were
the last of the Moors expelled from Spain?............77, 798, 82
Name three Mohammedan divisions which are now provinces
of Turkey... 20
In what countries does Mohammedanism now prevail?........ .717
What older styles of architecture were combined in the Saracenic?
Compare Moorish and Saracenic arches.................. 512

JAPAN

In what century were letters and the writings of Confucius first
known to Japan? From what country were they brought?.. 317
When was Buddhism introduced into Japan?.................. 124
Explain how the noble families of Japan came gradually to rule
the mikados... 124
At about what time did Japan adopt the feudal system? What
change of government was made in the 8th century?....124, 317
By whom were the Fujiwarra family opposed? Mention two other
families who came into power......................... 124
Give the name of the first shogun.......................... 124
Give the meaning of shogun. Compare the powers of the shogun
with the powers of the emperor, in the 12th century...... 124
What family controlled both the mikadoate and the shogunate
from 1199 to 1333?.................................... 124
Describe the influence of the Hojo family.................... 124
Whom did the Ashi-Kaga family succeed? What war did they
occasion?.. 124
State Japan's attitude towards feudalism at the time Europe was
discarding the feudal system........................... 124
Name a shogun who perfected marine architecture. What name
is given to the period in which he lived?.................. 124
When did Europeans begin to land in Japan? During what
year were all foreigners except Dutch and Chinese banished
from Japan?.. 124
Give an account of the religious strife in Japan between 1549 and
1615. Describe the effect upon Japan of its first hundred
years of intercourse with Christian nations............... 124
Give the name of the shogun under whom the Christians were
expelled from Japan.................................. 124

Upon what island were the Dutch traders confined?............ 124

To whom was the name Tycoon applied? At what time?....... 124

In what year did the American fleet under Commodore Perry visit
  Japan?..90, 124

When was the Perry treaty with the United States concluded?
  Why did the making of this treaty hasten the Japanese
  revolution?..124-125

What was the Dai Nihonshi? How did it affect the authority
  of the shogun? Trace a connection between this work and
  the revolution of the 19th century...................... 317

What changes in government followed the revolution of 1868? 125

By what country was Japan opened to the world after several
  European countries had failed in a similar attempt?........ 125

Give the date of the telegraph connection between Japan and
  Russia. When did Japan accept the European calendar?.95, 94

Why was Korea called the hermit nation? At what time did
  Korea make treaties with other nations?.................37-38

In what year did Japan adopt a constitution? Give the date
  of the first Japanese parliament.......................607, 95

Explain the cause of the war between China and Japan in 1894.
  Give the date and the terms of the treaty by which the war
  was ended..125, 164

In what year did the Russo-Japanese war begin? When did
  it end?... 139

What was the chief cause of. the Russo-Japanese war and what
  were some of the principal battles? In what place in the
  United States was the treaty closing this war signed? Mention
  the name of a noted American who did much to bring about
  this treaty..139, 153

Where is Port Arthur? Sketch briefly its history. Why was
  Port Arthur so important a point in the Russo-Japanese
  war?... 559

In what year did Korea pass under a Japanese protectorate?
  When did Japan annex Korea?....................38, 95, 125

Sketch briefly the lives of Togo, Oyama, and Oku. Which of
  these was called the Nelson of Japan?..................472-495

Give facts about Ito, Saionji, Takahira....................449-492

State facts about the educational system of Tokyo. What does
  the name Tokyo mean?...............................575, 844

How long did Emperor Mutsuhito rule? What progress did Japan
  make during his reign? Give date of his death............ 125

Name the present ruler of Japan. What is his official title?..... 605

What part did Japan take in the war of the nations?........... 125

CHINA

How long a period of time has elapsed since wheat, rice, tea, millet, the soy bean, and sorghum are known to have been in cultivation in China?............................... 55

When was silk culture begun in China?..................... 55

From what country and at what time was the manufacture of silk introduced into Europe?........................ 67

Who was Genghis Khan? What conquests did he make in the 13th century?................................35-36, 77, 436

By what ruler was the Mongol dynasty founded? In what year? What city did he build?........................36, 77

When was the Mongol dynasty expelled from China? By what dynasty were the Mongols succeeded?.................556, 36

When and by whom were the first authentic accounts of China written?... 36

Who were the Manchus? What dynasty did they establish? Give date.........:................................827, 36

Give the meaning of Peking. Of Nanking................... 834

When was the first British intercourse with China attempted? How did China treat the British merchants?.............. 36

In what year did Great Britain make war upon China?......... 36

Name five ports of China opened to British commerce in 1842. What other concessions were made to the British at that time?.. 36

Explain why the Tai-ping rebellion was so called. How did it result?... 36

During what years was China at war with Japan? State the results of the war....................................36, 139

Give some facts about the progress of China in commerce and science in the 19th century............................ 36

What was the Boxer rebellion?.........................30, 95, 36

When did China become a republic? Who became its president? 36

For how many years did the Manchus rule China? How long was China an empire?................................592, 36

State some facts in the life of Wu Ting-Fang................. 504

In what year did China declare war on Germany?............. 97

Who is president of China?................................. 605

LANGUAGE

Where does the Hamitic race belong, historically? What country was the center of the Hamitic civilization?....... **183**

In what region do the Semitic races first appear?.............. **183**

From what two sources has our knowledge of the Semitic language been chiefly drawn? By what means has our study of this subject been greatly aided?............................. **183**

What later civilization obscured that of the Hamitic race? Into what two classes are the Aryan tongues divided?.....**183, 184**

What name is given to the Aryan group that traveled farthest west? To which Aryan group does the Sanskrit language belong?.. **184**

Name the three great classes in which all languages originating on the eastern continents may be included..........**183-184**

To which of the three great divisions does the language of ancient Egypt belong? From which were the Hebrew and the Arabic developed? Which gave rise to the languages of modern Europe?....................................**183-184**

Into how many groups may the primitive languages of the American continent be divided?.............................. **183**

To whom was the British language indebted for its earliest words? Give some examples................................... **185**

By what people were the Celts succeeded in Britain? What changes did the Anglo-Saxons make in the language?... **185**

If the English language were divided into a hundred parts, how many parts would be of Anglo-Saxon origin? How many of Latin origin? How many of Greek origin?........... **185**

Which early tongue is called the basis of the English language?. **185**

From what source does the English derive most of its monosyllables? Verbs of action? Prepositions and numerals?. **185**

Explain why the English language is continually acquiring new words.. **185**

Name some words brought into Britain by the Romans. What sort of words did the introduction of Christianity bring into English?.. **185**

What did the Norman conquest do for the English language?.**185-186**

After the Norman conquest which classes retained the Saxon language? Which spoke French?........................ **185**

Contrast the names of ox, sheep, calf, deer when alive and when served as food. Account for the difference................ **186**

What sorts of words came to us from the Dutch? From which people did we get the language of chivalry, of law and government?..185-186

Name five words in our language of Dutch origin. Five of Latin origin. Five of Italian origin. Two of Danish origin..185-186

What characteristics are imparted to English by the German and the Latin?.. 186

What language is the principal source of our musical terms? Of our scientific terms? Of our dress and cooking terms? Of our military terms?.................................... 186

Mention five words the English acquired from the native Americans... 186

From what languages do we get the following words: shamrock, law, wagon, sing, pie, potato, conscience, telephone, piano, embroider, ask?......................................185-186

Give the preferred English plural of focus, syllabus. Which is the better English usage—*technic* or *technique? Grippe* or *grip?* 186

CAPITALS AND PUNCTUATION

Give five invariable rules for the use of capital letters. Illustrate each...187-188

When should *oh* begin with a capital? When the names of the points of the compass?...............................187-188

Should the names of the seasons be capitalized?............... 187

Which words in the titles of books should be capitalized?..... 187

Give the rule for the capitalization of titles of office or honor. When should such titles not begin with capitals? Give the rule for abbreviated titles.............................. 187

State the abbreviations for doctor of philosophy, doctor of laws, his majesty's service, fellow of the royal society, September. Punctuate each correctly..................202-207

What is the meaning of the wireless signal C. Q. D.?........ 203

Give the meaning of each of the following abbreviations and degrees: A. B., C. P. A., F. R. C. S., I. H. S., R. S. V. P., Xn., J. U. D.......................................202-208

What rule for capitals is applied when a title is used in place of a person's name?..................................... 187

In what cases should quotations begin with capitals? When should they not?.....................................187-188

What is the object of punctuation? Explain the difference between close and loose punctuation..................... 188

Show how changing the position of a comma may alter the meaning of a sentence.................................... 188

Give the names of the marks used for punctuation............. 188

In what two cases are periods always used?................... 188

State five rules for the use of the comma. Give an example of each...188-189

Illustrate the difference between a restrictive clause and a descriptive clause. How is the comma used with such clauses?.. 189

When should a subject clause be followed by a comma?....... 189

Compare the use of the semicolon with the use of the comma.. 189

When is the semicolon used between clauses joined by *for, but, and?* When is it used between the parts of a compound sentence?... 189

How do authorities differ in regard to the punctuation of sentences containing *as, viz., that is?*........................ 190

Give three illustrations of different rules for the use of the colon. 190

When should the interrogation point be used?................ 190

Explain the position of the interrogation point when used with quotation marks....................................... 190

When are the marks of parentheses used? When are brackets used? Give illustrations................................. 190

Show the use of the dash as a mark of punctuation by giving two illustrations....................................... 190

State three uses of the hyphen.............................. 190

What is the purpose of the double quotation marks? The single quotation marks? Illustrate each......................190-191

What is the present tendency in regard to the use of capitals and marks of punctuation?............................. 191

CORRECT USE OF WORDS

What is the correct pronunciation of the following words: address, adult, aeroplane, apparatus, chiropodist, clematis, clique, clothes, eczema?....................................267-270

Pronounce correctly the following: Anzac, Apache, Calais, Cleopatra, Danish, Eiffel, Goethals, Jekyll..................267-271

How should the following be pronounced: abdomen, acclimate, apricot, aunt, bicycle, frontier?........................267-271

Give the correct pronunciation of bouquet, calliope, clandestine, column, comparable, curator...........................268-270

Is your pronunciation of the following words correct: exit, exquisite, financier, frappé, genuine, mauve, meringue, modiste, vagary, vaudeville?...........................270-274

71

What is the meaning of *prima donna?* Give the correct pronunciation..266, 273

Give the correct pronunciation and the meaning of the following: apropos, chauffeur, coupé, décolleté, élite, passé, protégé, tête-à-tête, tout-ensemble, vis-à-vis.....................263-274

Do we *accept* or *except* invitations? Explain the correct use of *except* as compared with *besides* and *unless*.......191, 226, 254

Distinguish between being *almost* killed and being *nearly* killed.. 191

What are the correct uses of the words *alone* and *only?* Compare the meanings of *alone, solitary, lonely*...................191, 223

Give the exact meaning of *anticipate.* What is the difference between *prevent* and *anticipate?*........................192, 250

Correct the error in the following sentence: "I am anxious to have you live in New York." What different emotions are expressed by *distress* and *anxiety?*......................192, 237

Give sentences in which the following words are correctly used: *ability, capacity, talent*................................... 221

How does *intellect* differ from *talent?* What is the difference between *talent* and *genius?*............................. 246

When a man beats his horse, is the horse *abused* or *misused?*... 221

Which of the following is correct: "I am going to *make* a visit," or "I am going to *pay* a visit"?............................. 195

Should we say "Come *to* see me" or "Come *and* see me"?....... 191

What rule applies to the use of the words *farther* and *further?*... 194

Explain and illustrate the meaning of the words *emigrant* and *immigrant*... 193

In what kind of sentence should the connectives *so* and *as* be used together? When *as* and *as?*....................... 192

State the difference between a *dictionary,* a *lexicon,* and an *encyclopedia*... 236

Do we *cite* authors or do we *quote* them? Illustrate the distinction. 229

Are all authors writers? Are all writers authors? Explain.. 255

What is a *calamity?* A *disaster?* Was the San Francisco earthquake a calamity or a disaster? How do *calamity* and *loss* compare in meaning?................................227, 193

Do we differ *from* or *with* a person? Are certain things *different to* or *different from* other things?....................... 193

Compare the correct uses of the following words: *difference, variety; difference, distinction; difference, altercation*......... 236

How are the words *affect* and *effect* correctly used?.....193, 222, 238

Point out the error in this sentence: He had ought to go...... 194

Explain the distinction between the meanings of the words *character* and *reputation*................................... 229

Correct the following sentence: I know a widow woman in New York.. **198**

What is the difference between proclaiming and publishing? Use *proclaim* correctly in a sentence...................... **234**

What is wrong in this sentence: The individual left here on the last train?......................................194-195

To what do the words *fewer* and *less* apply? Illustrate their correct use.. **194**

Distinguish between *crime* and *vice* by using these words in sentences.. **233**

When do we *excuse* and when do we *pardon?* When do we *forgive?*...239, 242

Correct the error in the following sentence and give a reason for your answer: Those kind of apples are good......... **197**

What is the difference between *salary* and *wages?* Between *allowance* and *stipend?*....................................... **223**

How does an *axiom* differ from a *proverb?* What is an *adage?*. **225**

Correct the following sentences and give a reason for the correction: Leave me be. Leave me go............................ **195**

Show by sentences the correct use of the words *lie* and *lay* in the present tense. In the past tense. Correct the sentence: He laid upon the bed a long time........................ **195**

Contrast the meanings of the words *enough* and *sufficient*..... **239**

Explain the use of *learn* and *teach*. Point out the error in this sentence: I wish you would learn me to write.......:.... **195**

Do we *lend* money or do we *loan* it?.......................... **195**

Which has the highest authority, an *ambassador,* an *envoy* or a *plenipotentiary?* Explain their different functions........... **223**

What is the difference between *truth* and *veracity?*............. **254**

When do we *avenge* wrong and when do we *revenge* wrong?.... **192**

Is it possible for a person to be *civil* without being *polite?* Give a reason for your answer. What does *genteel* mean?....229, 242

Does your coat *sit* well or *set* well? Does the hen *set* on eggs or does she *sit* on eggs?................................. **196**

Explain clearly the use of the words *sit* and *set*. Give the origin of the saying that the sun sets........................... **196**

When do we *stop* at a hotel and when do we *stay* at a hotel?.. **197**

Is there any difference between *correction, discipline*, and *punishment?* Illustrate by using these words correctly in sentences... **233**

What word should generally be used instead of *lady?* What word is usually preferable to *gentleman?*.................... **195**

Distinguish between *error* and *fault*.......................... **239**

73

Which word in the following sentence is superfluous: A number
    of people congregated together in the hall?.............. 193
When do we *purchase* and when do we *buy?*.................. 196
Correct the error in this sentence: He lives on Jefferson street. 197
Explain the difference between *habitation* and *home.* Between
    house and *residence*...................................243-244
Do we die *of, with,* or *from* a certain disease?.................. 193
Distinguish between *contagion* and *infection.* Give the correct
    use of *contagious, epidemical, pestilential*.................. 232
When do we *cry* and when do we *weep?*...................... 234
Is a large tree *high* or *tall?* Is the bird's nest in the top of the
    tree *high* or *lofty?* Give a sentence in which *lofty* is correctly
    used... 244
What is wrong in this sentence: I took the medicine as a
    preventative?... 196
Give accurately the use of the following words: *business, occupa-
    tion, employment*.. 227
Distinguish between the meanings of *vocation* and *avocation*.. 227
Explain the difference between *increase* and *grow*.............. 246
Do we *smell* the rose or *smell of* the rose?...................... 197
Can a person be *conspicuous* without being *prominent?*......... 250
By what rule is the use of *can* and *may* governed? Illustrate by
    sentences in which *can* and *may* are correctly used......228, 195
Find the error in the sentence: She lives a long ways from the
    school.. 198
Do *ingenious* and *ingenuous* mean the same? Give a reason for
    your answer... 246
Give the difference between the words *intend* and *purpose.* Which
    is the stronger word, *purpose* or *design?*................195, 235
Show how *shall* and *will* are correctly used to express the future.
    How to express determination........................... 197
Give the exact meaning of the following sentence: We *will* go to
    the picnic tomorrow, rain or shine....................... 197
What does the following sentence mean: I *will* drown and
    nobody *shall* help me? Transpose *shall* and *will* and explain
    the meaning of the altered sentence...................... 197
Find the error in this sentence: The goods arrived all O. K.... 206
Correct the following sentences and give reasons for the cor-
    rections: (a) You may have all of it. (b) She had no
    money at all. (c) These hats are both just alike..........191-192
Do we put potatoes *in* the basket or *into* the basket? Is there
    any difference between walking *into* the room and walking
    in the room?.. 194

What rule is given for the use of the prepositions *in* and *into?*
Which of the two is sometimes an adverb?............... 194

Explain the difference between *audience* and *spectators.* Is it
correct to speak of the *audience* at a ball game?.......... 192

"I *calculate* to go away tomorrow." Correct the foregoing sentence, and explain what *calculate* means................193, 227

Do we write *all over* the page or *over all* the page?............. 191

Can one have a bad *temper* with a good *disposition?* Explain
your answer... 237

Why should we not say, "I expect you know all about it"? Give
the sentence correctly.................................. 194

Give the correct use of the words *beautiful, handsome, pretty.*
Is a handsome face always a pretty one? Would you call a
delicately colored flower handsome?...................... 226

"To the victors belong the spoils of the enemy." Is the foregoing statement justified by the meaning of the words *victor*
and *conqueror?*.. 232

Make a careful distinction between the meanings of *booty, spoil* and
prey. Use these words correctly in sentences............. 227

Do we *make* experiments or do we *try* them?................... 197

Do we *sustain* injuries or *receive* them?...................... 197

Distinguish between *cause, reason, motive.* Causes produce
effects. What do reasons and motives produce?........... 228

Is it permissible to end a sentence with a preposition?.......193-194

What is the difference between a person's *manners* and his *morals?*
Between his *air* and his *manner?* Illustrate the correct
use of these words....................................248, 223

LETTER WRITING

Name the six parts of a letter.............................. 214

What must the heading of a letter contain? Should the heading
be written on one line or on two lines? How should it be
punctuated?... 214

In dating a business letter what abbreviations are used for
January, February, and other months? Which months
are not abbreviated?................................202-207

On which line should the address begin? How should it be
written? Should the word *street* or *avenue* in the address
begin with a capital?................................... 214

Give three forms of salutation for a formal letter. What is the
most formal salutation? To whom is it addressed? Is a
complimentary salutation used for the president of the
United States?... 214

Why is it proper to write "My dear Mr. Jones" to a stranger? Which is regarded as the more formal address—"Dear Mr. Brown" or "My dear Mr. Brown"?...................... 214

What word of the salutation must always be capitalized? State the difference of opinion in regard to the capitalization of its other words.....................................214-215

How should the salutation be punctuated? Why should the dash not be used?...................................... 215

On what line should the body of the letter begin? Where should a margin be left? How wide should the margin be?.. 215

What is meant by the complimentary close? Where should it be written? Give a rule for its capitals and punctuation. 215

Name the forms of complimentary closing used in business correspondence. What forms should be used when the writer intends to show respect?.......................... 215

Where should the signature be written? If one wishes to sign "Miss" or "Mrs." to a business letter, within what marks should such words be inclosed?.......................... 215

What is the address on the envelope called?................... 215

Of how many lines does the superscription usually consist? In what order are they arranged? Where should the first line be written?...................................... 215

How should the superscription be punctuated? Are commas to be used on the envelope?............................. 215

What title is prefixed to the name of a clergyman? To what persons is the term "honorable" applied? How is it abbreviated?...215-216

Should a degree, such as LL.D., be written after a man's name, if Hon. has been used before the name?................... 216

Correct these errors: Hon. Judge Boyd, Rev. Jones. Is it permissible to address a letter to Mrs. Dr. Brown?........... 216

Give the exact form for the outside and the inside of a letter addressing the president of the United States. How is the governor of the state to be addressed?................. 216

Give general rules for business letters. How long may a business letter remain unanswered?............................. 216

Distinguish fully between a business letter and a friendly letter.
....216-217, 219-220

How may a letter of recommendation be addressed? Write a letter of recommendation............................... 217

In what person are formal invitations always written? In what person should the reply to a formal invitation be written? Give an example of a formal invitation...............218-219

Write a letter of application. A note of introduction. An informal invitation...............................217-219
For what purposes may a post card be used? Is it permissible to write a personal message on a post card?............... 220

HIGHER ENGLISH

Account for the origin of figurative language. What is a figure of speech?...208-209
Make three literal statements. Express the same thoughts in figurative language...................................... 209
Define figure of grammar. Figure of rhetoric. When we speak of figurative language do we usually mean figures of grammar or figures of rhetoric?...........................209-210
Name the classes into which figures of grammar are divided. How many figures of orthography are mentioned? How many of etymology? How many of syntax?..................209-210
Give an illustration of each of the figures of orthography..... 209
What are figures of etymology? What sorts of changes are made in words by these figures?........................209-210
What is a figure of syntax? Name two principal figures of syntax and give an illustration of each.......................... 210
Into how many classes are figures of rhetoric divided? On what is each of the first four based?.............................. 210
Name the figures based on resemblance. Give two examples of simile. Of metaphor.................................210-211
By what words is the comparison in simile usually introduced? Which are the best similes?............................. 210
How does a metaphor differ from a simile? Give sentences to show the difference. Illustrate two grades of metaphors.......210-211
Which figure of speech is more commonly used than any other?. 211
Compare personification with metaphor. Define personification. Give an example................................. 211
What is allegory? Discuss the resemblance between allegory, metaphor, and simile. State two marked differences between the metaphor and the allegory........................... 211
Mention two well-known allegories. Name their authors. Outline the story of each............................211, 374, 376
Point out and name the figures based on resemblance which are found in the following sentences: "Experience keeps a dear school, but fools will learn in no other." "Falsehood is cowardice—truth is courage." "He had a face like a benediction."...210-211

Give the names of the figures based on contiguity. Define each.. 211

Name six varieties of metonymy. Give an example of each variety.. 211

State what kind of metonymy is used in each of the following sentences: (a) Do you enjoy Dickens? (b) Our flag must be respected. (c) The battleships opened fire at Vera Cruz. (d) The fisherman's net was drying in the sun..... 211

How does synecdoche differ from metonymy? Give an illustration.. 211

State whether synecdoche or metonymy is employed in the following sentence: "Shoot, if you must, this old gray head.".. 211

How many figures are based on contrast or surprise? Name and define three of them.............................211-212

Give three examples of antithesis. Of epigram. To which class does the pun belong?............................ 212

What is irony? Quote a famous passage illustrating this figure of speech.. 212

To what class of figures does hyperbole belong? Name three other figures belonging to the same class................212-213

Give an example of hyperbole. What is the effect of the frequent use of this figure?................................. 212

Explain the following figures and give an example of each: exclamation, apostrophe, vision..........................212-213

Tell what figure of speech is used in each of the following sentences: "Give us this day our daily bread." "How dear to my heart are the scenes of my childhood!" "Fools rush in where angels fear to tread." "Roll on, thou deep and dark blue ocean—roll!" "Waves mountain high washed the boat ashore." "The more haste, the less speed." "Thrilling tales told to tiny tots."......................211-213

Distinguish clearly between climax and anticlimax. In what class of writing is anticlimax often used?....... 213

Define euphemism, onomatopœia, alliteration. Give illustrations of each... 213

Name two types of composition. Compare the language of prose with the language of poetry........................ 198

What are the chief varieties of prose composition? What does each accomplish?....................................... 198

State the aim of narration. Mention nine forms of writing that may be classed under narration.................... 198

What is a plot? How do letters, memoirs, and biographies differ from stories, novels, and dramas?....................... 198

Name some books of travel and their authors. What books of travel have been written by Frank G. Carpenter? John Muir? Theodore Roosevelt?...................198, 416-482

What is the difference between biography and autobiography? How do memoirs differ from biography? Mention a well-known autobiography. What biographies did Washington Irving write?..198, 448

How does history differ from memoirs? From biography? Name some well-written histories......................198-199

What is the aim of fiction? Name at least six forms of fiction. What educational value have the best novels?............ 199

Explain the difference between a myth and a fable. Between a parable and an allegory............................... 199

What are folk-tales and legends? To what form of composition do they belong? Name some well-known writers of short, stories, and mention some of their best-known works..... 199

Of what may description treat? Which is easier—to describe external objects or to delineate character? Mention three celebrated writers who have excelled in description of character..198, 199-200

How is description related to narration? In what respect does exposition differ from both description and narration? Name five forms of exposition.....................199, 200, 198

Distinguish between an editorial and an essay. Between a review and a criticism. Name three writers of notable essays... 200

What is the purpose of argumentative discourse? Of what steps does such a discourse consist? How does it differ from a debate?.. 200

Into what classes of composition is persuasion divided? State the aim of persuasion. How does the appeal made by persuasion differ from the appeal made by argumentation and exposition?... 200

How does a lecture differ from a sermon? From an oration? From an address?...................................... 200

Mention two celebrated orations. What rank does the oration occupy in prose composition?............................ 200

Name the three parts into which orations, addresses, and speeches are divided... 200

What are the three kinds of arguments used in a sermon? Of how many parts does a sermon consist?................200-201

Into how many groups is poetry divided? Name them....... 198

Explain how poetry differs from prose, mentioning form, language, and aim... 201

79

What is the character of epic poetry? Name some of the great epics and their authors.................................. 201

To what class of poetry do "Evangeline" and the "Lay of the Last Minstrel" belong? Name others of the same class... 201

Give an outline of the "Faerie Queene". Of "The Lay of the Last Minstrel"..357, 366

How do the ballad and the tale differ from the epic and metrical romances?......... 201

To what class of poetry do "Robin Hood" and "Chevy Chase" belong? Tell something about these poems.........201, 378, 350

What are the characteristics of dramatic poetry? Before the age of Shakespere, what was the highest form of dramatic art? Who were the dramatists of Pericles' time?....198, 201

What are the chief divisions of the drama? Distinguish between tragedy and comedy..................................... 201

Outline the plot of "Hamlet". Of "Macbeth". By whom were these written? To what class of dramatic poetry do they belong?..361, 369, 201

Mention five well-known comedies. Give the names of the authors.. 201

Give a brief sketch of "Pippa Passes." Of "Merchant of Venice." Of "Midsummer Night's Dream." Which of Shakespere's plays are called his fairy plays?.....201, 376, 371

What is the story of "The Tempest"? Of "She Stoops to Conquer"? Name the author of each..................383, 382

How does opera differ from drama? What is melodrama? Name the author and composer of the world's greatest operas... 201

What classes of poems belong to the lyric group? Mention a lyric poem by Ben Jonson. By Tennyson. By Burns. 201, 390, 202

Distinguish the ode from other poetic forms. Mention some English odes. Give the first line of Milton's "Hymn on the Nativity." Wordsworth's "Ode on Immortality."...201-202, 389

What is the nature of an elegy? Mention three elegies. Give their first lines....................................202, 387-389

Of how many lines does a sonnet consist? What are its themes? Name three English poets who have written sonnets...... 202

Mention a sonnet by Richard Watson Gilder. Quote its first line..202, 214

Compare didactic poetry with other poetic forms. Give the title of one didactic poem..................................... 202

Account for the popularity of lyric poems.................... 202

What form of poetry is "Essay on Man"? "In Memoriam"? "Lead, Kindly Light"?................................. 202

LITERATURE

What is literature, and what is its kindred science?.......... 277

Compare literature and history. Show how the two are closely affiliated... 277

By what manner of study can any single literature be best understood?.. 277

Name seven ancient oriental literatures...................... 277

Into what three periods may the development of early literatures be divided?... 277

Between 2000 B. C. and 1500 B. C. what was the character of inscriptions made in Babylonia and Assyria? In Egypt?. 277

Compare the golden age of Babylonian literature with the literary conditions of China and Arabia during the same period.. 277

When and by whom were letters first used in Egypt? Who invented the Egyptian alphabet?........................... 55

Give items showing the degree of civilization of Egypt in the 20th and 19th centuries B. C............................ 55

Sketch the progress of literature during the period from 1500 B. C. to 1000 B. C. Compare the literature of Egypt with that of Babylon and the Hebrews........................ 277

After the year 1000 B. C. what literatures began to decline? Compare the literary activity of China during the 500 years following 1000 B. C. with that of India, Arabia, and Persia.. 277

In what year did Cyrus the Persian conquer Babylonia? Compare this conquest with the period of decline of Babylonian literature......................................58, 277

In all literatures which appeared earlier—prose or verse?........ 294

To the literature of what country does the oldest temperance ode in the world belong?................................. 278

ANCIENT ORIENTAL LITERATURES

Give a brief description of the extent of the literature of India. 277

Name five languages included in the Indo-European group. How is the Sanskrit related to this group?..................; 277

Which is the most ancient of the Hindu literatures?............ 277

Which of the oriental literatures is supposed to bear the closest resemblance to the primitive language?.................... 277

Give an account of the Sanskrit, stating to whom it is a sacred language, by whom it is now written and spoken, and naming the earliest form in which Sanskrit appears. 277, 380

What does Veda mean? Divide the Vedas into four classes. Of what does each class consist? State the two parts of each Veda... 277

Explain the meaning of Vedanga. What does Vedanga include?.277-278

What is the code of Manu? The Mahabharata? The Ramayana? To what times do these writings belong?................278, 277

When and by whom was Buddhism founded? What are the sacred books of Buddha called? In what language are they written?..278, 689

In what country did many of the fairy tales told in English-speaking homes originate?.............................. 278

In the Hindu mythology who were Vishnu, Brahma, Siva? What does the word avatar mean?.........................342, 326

Give the legend of Rahu. Who were the Rakshasas?........... 340

By what name is the earliest language of Persia known? To what other language is it allied? What are the evidences that the people of India and those of Persia were originally one community?....................................... 278

Name some countries in which cuneiform letters were employed. What are cuneiform letters?.....................278, 277, 351

What is the nature of the Zend-Avesta? When was it compiled? State the position it occupies among Indo-European literatures..278, 277

Whom do the Persians regard as the author of the Zend-Avesta? Of what does the Avesta consist, and in what manner was it brought together? What is known of the life of Zoroaster? 278, 504

When did Alexander the Great conquer Persia? What effect had his conquest upon the language and the literature of the Persians?..60, 278

During what period did modern Persian literature flourish? How does it compare with the literature of ancient Persia?... 278

Mention three later Persian writers—a great moral teacher, a court historian, and a writer of lyric poems,............ 278

What position did Firdausi occupy? For what is Omar Khayyam celebrated? Tell some facts about each............278, 433, 472

Mention the chief hero of the Persian romances. Sketch the story of his life.. 379

Give the Persian myths of Ormuzd, Ahriman, Mithras, the ferohers...324-337

How complete is the literature of ancient China? What writings were preserved in the sacred books?...................... 278

Name the first book published in China. What is known of this
book and of its original date?............................ 279
At how early a date was a dictionary of Chinese compiled?.... 56
What is the "Book of History"? The "Book of Rites"? By
whom were they compiled?.............................. 279
What are the "Four Books"? By whom were they written?
What was the influence of the "Five Classics" and the "Four
Books" upon Chinese thought and life?.................. 279
During what century did Confucius live? Mention three impor-
tant facts concerning his life........................... 422
Who was Laotse? Of whom was he a contemporary? For what
writings is he celebrated?.............................. 455
Who has been called the Plato of China? Of whom was he a
follower? State one of his teachings. What was his method
of discussion? What is the Mengtse?................279, 370
What effect has the educational system of the Chinese produced
upon their students?................................... 279
Give an account of the poetry of China. In what form are official
documents sometimes issued?............................ 279
What three philosophies are found in China? Mention some other
classes of works predominant in Chinese literature....... 279
Which literature stands first among the literatures of antiquity?. 279
Account for the universal significance of Hebrew literature. Of
what sort of people is it the story?....................... 279
Mention some of the characteristics of Hebrew literature and
Hebrew law... 279
In what form has the most important part of Hebrew literature
been preserved? During what period were these books
written? Prior to that time how was knowledge of Hebrew
history preserved?.................................279-280
What is the prevalent idea of Hebrew literature? Contrast
the Hebrew conception of God with the divinities of other
nations... 280
Outline the four periods into which Hebrew literature is divided. 280
Sketch the life of Moses, tracing the progress of the Hebrews
under his guidance..................................468, 55
Name the books included in the Hebrew pentateuch. To what
writer are they ascribed? Outline the subject matter of
each book..280, 375
What book of the Bible is older than the books of Moses?....... 277
Give the names of the historic books of the Bible. Of the poetic
books. Of the books of wisdom.....................280-281

Sketch the lives of David and Solomon. To what class of Hebrew
  literature do their writings belong?...............425, 489, 281
Who are the major Hebrew prophets? How many minor prophets
  are there?... 281
State facts about Isaiah, Jeremiah, Ezekiel, Daniel..........424-450
What was the period of the Babylonian captivity? What name
  is given to the literature of the Hebrews from the epoch
  of the captivity?...................................57-58, 280
To what writings is the name rabbinical literature applied?
  What are its characteristics? What is the septuagint?..280, 381
Divide the books of the new testament into four classes.... 281
Name the authors of the four biographical books. Give addi-
  tional books of the new testament written by some of these
  men. Which wrote the history of the acts of the apostles?
  ....281, 451-463
How does an epistle differ from a letter? To whom were the
  Pauline epistles addressed? Outline the life of St. Paul.
  ....247, 281, 474
What is the apocalypse? Who is said to have written it?..281, 345
How many books are there in the old testament? How many in
  the new testament?...................................280-281
Briefly describe the Talmud. Mention its two great divisions.280, 383
Mention three celebrated schools for the study of rabbinical
  literature... 280
Compare the material on which the Persians wrote with that used
  by the Babylonians. What sort of inscriptions indicate
  a common origin for these two races?.................. 281
What is the oldest known specimen of Chaldean writing? What
  is the oldest Chaldean book?.......................... 281
What were the famous tile libraries of Babylon? What subjects
  did the works in these libraries cover?............... 281
What effect did the decline of Babylon have on the literature
  of Assyria?.......................................281, 277
Describe the library at Nineveh. When was it destroyed?... 281
Under what ruler did Babylon build up a great library? What
  became of it?.....................................281, 128
Mention some valuable records recovered from the libraries of
  Babylon and Nineveh. In what form are these records?.. 281
Why did the literature of Arabia develop slowly? Before the
  7th century what was the character of Arabian literature?. 281
What poetic contests were held in Arabia in the 4th and 5th
  centuries? Mention the chief characteristics of the Arabian
  poets.. 281

State the influence of Mohammed on the advancement of learn-
ing in Arabia during the 7th and 8th centuries.......... 282
Name a great religious work written by Mohammed. What
was its aim?..467, 282
What centuries are included in the golden age of Arabian letters?
Who ruled at that time?.............................. 282
Name three of the leading Arabian universities of the 8th century.
Mention some of the studies encouraged by them.......... 282
Who was Avicenna? What did he write? To what study did
Averrhoës devote his life?...........................402, 401
Why is Arabic studied extensively by modern scholars?......... 282
Give the meaning of the following according to Arabian mytho-
logy: peri, Eblis, Azrael.............................326-339
What are meant by Al-sirat, Israfil, sedrat?................324-341
Of what do the remains of early Egyptian literature consist?.. 282
During what centuries were hieroglyphic characters used in
Egypt? What forms of writing succeeded the hieroglyphic?. 282
What discovery about the close of the 18th century simplified
the study of ancient Egyptian literature?.............282, 378
Mention three religious works of the early Egyptians. Name
a moral treatise contemporaneous with the "Book of the
Dead"...282, 277
What was the golden age of Egyptian literature?............... 277
Give the title of the oldest fairy story in the world and tell how
long ago it was written.............................. 282

GREEK LITERATURE

Name three traditional poets of ancient Greece. Sketch some
of the early legends of Greece........................... 283
What were the twelve labors of Hercules? How does Hercules
rank among the Grecian heroes? What was his distinguishing characteristic?..................................... 331
Describe the expedition of the argonauts. The ship in which
they sailed... 325
Tell something about Jason, Castor and Pollux, Theseus, Colchis,
the golden fleece, Medea.........................326-342, 325
In what period did Homer live? From what war do his two
great poems date? Which poem is called the beginning
of literature?..................................282-283, 446
State some theories in regard to the authorship of the Homeric
poems. Give the traditions of Homer's life.............446-447
What two poems are the foundation of Grecian literature? To
what class of poetry do they belong?..................283, 201

When was the Iliad written? Of how many books does it consist? What does it commemorate?....................... 363

Give the mythical history of Paris, Helen, Menelaus. Outline the story of the Iliad............................331-338, 363

According to the Iliad what parts did the following play in the Trojan war—Agamemnon, Hector, Achilles, Priam? 324-340, 363

Tell the story of the Odyssey. By what other name is Ulysses known? Describe the characters of Ulysses and Penelope. 373, 342, 339

In what ways were Calypso, Circe, Telemachus, Nestor, and Mentor connected with the wanderings of Ulysses?.373, 326-341

Why were the cyclic poets so called? When did they flourish? What do their poems recount?.......................... 283

State the time at which Hesiod lived. What are his two representative poems? Contrast his works with those of Homer...282, 283

By what name are poems that aim to teach known? What is the theme of Hesiod's "Works and Days"? Of his "Theogony"?...202, 283

During what period was the epic the only poetic form used in Greece? Explain how the republican movement in Greece led to the development of the elegy and the epigram.... 283

Name the author of some Greek elegies. When did Thales live and what did he write?......................283, 282, 494

During what centuries did Æsop live? What is the character of his writings? Tell what is known of his life.........283, 394

What is meant by the seven wise men? Who were they?.381, 283, 116

What is the character of the lyric poems of Greece? Mention three writers of lyrics. Which is the greatest?..........283, 282

Give some facts about Anacreon. To what sort of verse is the term anacreontic applied?............................397, 344

Mention the founders of three schools of Greek philosophy. What was the teaching of each school?.................... 284

Sketch the lives of Anaxagoras, Anaximander, and Diogenes. To what school of philosophy did they belong? Which opened the first school of philosophy at Athens?.....397-427, 284

Mention three noted Greeks who were pupils of Anaxagoras..... 397

At about what time did Pythagoras live? Mention three of his doctrines. When did Zeno live? When was the stoic school of philosophy founded?...................284, 479, 504

How did Grecian drama originate? Who is known as the founder of dramatic art?.. 284

Mention three of the greatest writers of Greek tragedy. What Greek writer holds the highest place as a writer of comedy?. 284

Give facts about Æschylus, Sophocles, Euripedes and Aristophanes. Under which did Greek drama reach its highest excellence?...................................284, 394-489

Who was the first Greek writer of history? Name two other great Greek historians and compare their styles of writing. 284

Sketch the lives of Herodotus, Thucydides, and Xenophon. Which is called the father of history? What did Thucydides write? What historic retreat is the subject of Xenophon's Anabasis?...................................445-504, 284

Name five Greek orators. Which established a school of political oratory? What two of these were rivals?........... 284

Give an account of the lives of Demosthenes and Æschines. 426, 394

At what time was Socrates born? What was his early occupation? To what great work was much of his life devoted? How did Socrates' philosophy differ from that of his predecessors?...................................489, 284

Through the writings of which of Socrates' pupils are the principles of Socrates best expressed?........................ 284

Of whom was Plato a pupil? What are the characteristics of Plato's writings? Give an account of his life. What is Plato's "Phædo"? His "Republic"?..........477, 284, 375, 377

Who was the teacher of Aristotle? How was he described by that teacher? Tell something of Aristotle's philosophic work...................................399, 284

Who founded the epicurean school of philosophy? What are its teachings? Of what school did it become a rival?..284, 431

In what century did Euclid lay the foundation for modern geometry? What is known of his life?.................284, 431

What did Archimedes write? In what scientific field was he a brilliant inventor? What do modern engineers owe to Archimedes?...................................283, 399, 284

Who conquered Greece in 146 B. C.? What effect had this conquest on the literature of Greece?....................62, 284

Name some of the writers of Greece after the Roman conquest. 284

For what work is Plutarch celebrated? To what school of philosophy did he belong?............................477, 284

In what century did Epictetus teach? What position did he occupy during early life?............................431, 284

According to Greek mythology who were the Titans, Kronos, and Cybele?...................................342, 333, 327

How was the government of the world divided among Zeus, Poseidon, and Hades? What part did each obtain?........ 342

Where did Zeus live? What was the extent of his power?.... 342

What important position does each of the following gods occupy in Greek mythology: Aphrodite, Apollo, Ares, Artemis, Bacchus, Demeter, Hera, Hermes, Hestia, Pallas-Athene?.325-338

Over what did each of the following gods preside: Æolus, Æsculapius, Eos, Helios, Iris, Nemesis, Nox, Pan, Plutus, Themis?...324-341

Where was the palace of Poseidon? Over what did he rule?.. 340

Who was Triton? What were Scylla and Charybdis, the hydra, naiads, nereids, Oceanus, sirens?......................327-342

Who was Hades? What was the ensign of his power? What blessings did he give?...............................330-331

Where was the river Lethe? To what region was the name Erebus applied? Who was Cerberus?.............334, 329, 327

Describe the rivers Styx, Cocytus, Acheron. Who was Charon? 324, 327, 341

What were the duties of the Eumenides? Fates? Harpies? Nemesis?...329-336

Name the nine muses and tell over what each one presided. Where did they live?.................................... 336

Give the legend connected with each of the following: Clytie, Daphne, Echo, Hyacinthus, Iris, Lotis, Narcissus........327-336

How did the Greeks immortalize Andromeda, Casseopeia, Castor and Pollux (Gemini), Orion, Pleiades, Sirius?.....325-341

Tell the story of one exploit of Perseus and one of Bellerophon as found in the following references: Perseus, helmet of Hades, Medusa, Pegasus, Hippocrene, Bellerophon, Pirene, the chimæra..326-339

Who was Theseus? Associate the following with one of his adventures: Minos, Dædalus, the minotaur, Ariadne..342, 325-336

What and where is each of the following: Castaly, Delphi, Elysium, Helicon, Olympus, Parnassos, Pelion?..........326-339

Tell something of Adonis, Antæus, Arachne, Atlas, Briareus, Cadmus, Chiron, Hygeia, Orpheus, Phaeton.............324-339

LATIN LITERATURE

What is the character of the first writings of the Romans? Compare with the early literature of other nations....... 285

In what wars was Rome engaged between 264 and 146 B. C.? How did this affect the intellectual condition and the literature of the Romans?................................138, 285

Whose name comes first in the literature of Rome? What was his nationality?... 285

What great change in Roman customs was instituted by Livius Andronicus? In what year? How long were his writings used as texts in the Roman schools?........................ 285

Name two great comic poets of Rome. Mention one work of each...285, 284

Who is known as the father of Latin song? When did he live? What did he write?.................................285, 284

Against what were the satires of Lucilius directed? Who invented the word satire?....................................... 285

Give an account of Cato as a writer and as a Roman citizen. What was the nature of his greatest work?................ 285

Mention five noted Latin authors who wrote during the 1st century B. C.......................................284, 285

What influence did Cicero exert on the Latin language? What was the varied character of his writings?................285, 284

At what age did Cicero begin to speak in public? What offices did he fill? What conditions led to his proscription and death?... 419

Explain the patriotic act which earned for Cicero the title of father of his country.................................... 419

What was the object of Catiline's conspiracy? What was the result of his attempt to execute his plans?................ 417

Sketch the life of Julius Cæsar, showing conquests made by him. Of what do his commentaries consist?..............414, 63, 285

What was the nature of Lucretius' writing? State the cause of his death... 460

Name three works of Sallust. Why are they valuable? What was Sallust's literary style?.......................284, 285, 485

For what is the Augustan age of Roman literature distinguished? Mention four writers of the Augustan age................. 285

When did Virgil live? How does he rank among the Augustan poets? Name three of his works and state the character of each...284, 285, 497

Give an outline of Virgil's Æneid. At what point does it take up the tale related by Homer in the Iliad? Who is Æneas? Anchises?................................343, 363, 324, 325

What are the "Georgics" of Virgil?............................ 359

Compare the date of birth of Horace with the birth date of the Roman emperor Augustus...........................284, 146

Name three works written by Horace. State why they are attractive to cultivated minds........................285, 447

Who was Cornelius Nepos? In what regard is his only extant
work held?.......................................284, 470

By what name did Livy call his history of Rome? Compare
Livy with other historians. Tell something of his life..458, 285

What did Ovid write?....................................... 285

To what school of philosophy did Seneca belong? Name some
of his works. Give three other facts about the life of Seneca.487, 285

Mention a work written by Pliny the Elder. By Quintilian... 285

Outline the principal events in the life of Tacitus. Name his
chief works..492, 285

What conditions gave rise to the satires of Juvenal? Did Juvenal
live before or after the beginning of the Christian era?..285, 452

Through the influence of what conditions did Latin literature
come to an end?....................................... 285

Mention five of the Latin fathers of the church. What philosophy
did they follow? Give some facts about the lives and writings of St. Ambrose, St. Augustine, St. Jerome..285-286, 396-450

Which of the Latin fathers wrote the "Te Deum Laudamus"?
Which made the Latin translation of the Bible known as
the Vulgate?...........................:........396, 450, 386

Arrange in the order in which they lived: Horace, Virgil, Cicero,
Ovid, Tacitus, Livy..................................284-285

According to Roman mythology over what did Jupiter, Neptune,
and Pluto preside? Which of these corresponds to the
Greek Zeus? Poseidon? Hades?.....................330-342

What relation did each of the following bear to Jupiter: Juno,
Minerva, Latona, Apollo, Diana?......................325-335

For what qualities were Apollo and Minerva celebrated? Who
introduced the worship of Diana into Rome? In which
two of these were the sun and the moon deified?....325, 335, 328

Over whom did Saturn and Janus rule? What place had each
of the following in the life of the Roman people: Ceres,
Mars, Mercury, Pax, Pluvius, Vesta, Vulcan?..........327-342

Relate the mythological tale of Venus, Cupid, and Psyche.342, 327, 340

What was personified in each of the following: Aurora, Flora,
Fortuna, Luna, Morpheus, Nox, Somnus?................326-341

What were the Parcæ? How many were there? What was their
power over the life of man?............................. 338

SCANDINAVIAN LITERATURE

In earliest literature to what people is the term Scandinavian
applied? Until about what time was Icelandic the literary
language of all the Scandinavians? What name do the
earliest authorities give to this language?...............286, 288

How does the early Scandinavian poetry compare with that of other Teutonic races? Describe the poetry of the early Scandinavian literature 286

Of what form of poetry was the saga the outgrowth? To what century does the saga in its purest form belong? When was it lost in biography? 286

What does the word Edda mean and to what is it applied? Of what does the "elder" Edda treat? The "younger" Edda? By whom and when was each compiled? 286, 379, 354

Who was the greatest Scandinavian writer of the 12th and 13th centuries? 286

During what century did Swedish literature begin? Name two of the earliest writings 286, 287

Of what did St. Bridget's revelations consist? When did she live ? 286, 287

By whom was the Bible translated into Swedish? 286, 287

In what form does the earliest Swedish poetry appear? When was the first book printed in Swedish? 286

Mention two brothers who studied under Luther. What did they write? How was Swedish literature affected by the reformation? 286, 287

How did Buræus arouse interest in Scandinavian language and mythology? Who ruled Sweden at that time? 286

During whose reign did the Swedish drama begin? Who is the greatest Swedish dramatist? 286

Give facts about the life of Messenius. Mention his first comedy and his first tragedy 286-287

Who was the father of Swedish poetry? Give an account of his writings, showing their influence on Swedish literature. 287

What is the character of the writings of Gustavus Adolphus? Who was he? 287, 83

What discoveries made Rudbeck famous? With what university was he connected? State the name and the object of his greatest work. Characterize his writings 287

Who was Emanuel Swedenborg? What is the nature of his writings? When did he live? 492

In what year was Linnæus born? What was the chief interest of his life? Mention one of his works 457

What author shows the English and the French influence upon 18th century Swedish literature? Name two of his writings. After what English authors are they modeled? 287

When was Dalin born? Compare with the dates of birth of Addison and Pope. Name three other English contemporaries of Dalin 287, 296

What writer is known as the Swedish Sappho?................ 287

Mention three poets born in 1740, 1772, 1779, respectively.
Which of these is called the Anacreon of Sweden?......287, 405

In what field are the writings of Berzelius? When did he live?
With what university was he connected?.................. 406

What was the nature of the Swedish academy? The object of
the Gothic society? Name two famous writers connected
with the new school of literature...................... 287

Under what pseudonym did King Oscar II write? Mention two
of his works... 472

Give the names of four Swedish writers of history. Which of
these was the legal historian?........................... 287

Name two Swedish women who wrote poems. One who wrote
novels... 287

What was the year of August Strindberg's birth? Of his death?
Name his greatest work............................... 287

Mention two books of travel by Hedin. Sketch the life of the
author... 444

Between what centuries were the Danish ballads probably composed? How much later is the language in which they are
preserved?.. 288

In what period did Danish literature begin? Mention a writer
of that time. What did he write?....................288, 373

What did Tycho Brahe write? In what country did he spend
most of his life?....................................288, 411

Who was the first original dramatist in Denmark? Who is
called the founder of Danish poetry?..................... 288

What did Holberg write? Wessel? Ewald? Oehlenschläger?...... 288

Name one Danish author who wrote a medical work. One who
wrote on zoölogy. One on geography................... 288

Where and when was Hans Christian Andersen born? What
is the nature of his writings?...................288-289, 397

Mention a Danish writer of the latter half of the 19th century.. 289

When was the first book printed in Norway? By whom?....... 289

Who was the earliest original writer in Norway?.............. 289

By whom was "The Dawn of Norway" written? For what
purpose?... 289

Name the two compilers of a collection of old Norse folk-tales.
How was their material gathered?....................... 289

In what year was Ibsen born? What are three of his best-
known dramas?...................................448, 289

Name Björnson's leading works. What honor was conferred
upon him by Norway?............................289, 407

In the Norse mythology who was Alfadur? Give the legend of Ginungagap and Midgard........................324, 330, 335

Who were the Æsir? What were Asgard, Bifrost, Glasir?.324, 325-330

What is the connection between Heimdal, Ragnarok, and Lif? 331, 340, 334

Who were the Valkyrs? What was Valhalla? Tell something about the Gjallar bridge and the Gjallar horn...........342, 330

Relate the tradition of Odin................................. 337

Associate each of the following with Odin: Frigga, Thor, Balder, Bragi, Iduna. Who were Frey, Freya, Frodi, Hymir, Loki?..326-342

To what source does Grimm attribute the tale of the sleeping beauty?.. 382

GERMAN LITERATURE

Mention two of the oldest poems in German literature. To what remote times may these poems be traced? Give a brief outline of "Reynard the Fox".........................290, 377

Sketch the progress of learning in Germany during the reign of Charles the Great and Louis the Pious. By whom was the writing of that time chiefly done?..................... 290

What is the first novel in modern European literature? When and by whom was it written?.........................290, 289, 378

In what language were the histories of the 11th century written? 290

Who became the leaders of literature in Germany about 1200? In what class of writings did they excel?................... 291

Name three great poets of the 12th and 13th centuries....... 291

What name is generally applied to the Nibelungenlied? Into how many parts is the poem divided? What is its principal theme?..372, 291

Who were King Nibelung, Siegfried, Kriemhild, dwarf Alberich, Hagen, Brunhild, Etzel?............................348-382

Mention another epic similar to the Nibelungenlied..........291, 361

Tell the story of Parsifal. Of Lohengrin. Who wrote them?.374, 367

Outline the legend of Tannhäuser. What German composer made Tannhäuser the subject of an opera?............. 383

Through what orders of monks did preaching become a powerful educational influence? By whom was the mystic school founded? Who were the greatest writers of the 14th and 15th centuries?.. 291

Give an account of the life and writings of Thomas à Kempis.453, 291

In what century did modern German literature begin? Name four writers of that century............................. 291

What were the principal works of Martin Luther and Ulrich von Hutten?....................................291, 460, 289

What did Hans Sachs write? When and by whom was the German drama founded?..............................291, 80

What was the effect of the thirty years' war on German literature?... 291

In whose reign did German literature revive?.................. 291

Who were Klopstock and Herder? What did they write? What is Klopstock's "Messiah"?........................291, 290, 371

Tell something of the life of Lessing. Name three of his works. Which one stimulated historic study in Germany? Which was a treatise on art?...........................457, 290, 291

Outline the influence of the philosophy of Kant on modern thought. Name three of his works. What name has since been applied to his doctrines?....................452-453, 291

What was the principle of Fichte's philosophy?................ 291

Give an account of the life of Goethe. Mention four of his well-known works. What is the object of Goethe's "Wilhelm Meister"?......................................438, 291, 370

Briefly describe the character Faust. Mephistopheles........357, 335

With what other European writers does Goethe rank? To whose influence did Goethe owe much of his success?....... 291

What made Weimar the center of intellectual life during the latter part of the 18th century?.......................... 291

Relate the important events in the life of Schiller. Mention two of his historical works. Five of his dramas.......486, 291

What is the greatest drama in the German language? By whom was it written?....................................... 291

Name three poets who were contemporaries of Schiller. What did each write?.....................................291-292

Give the names of three works by Jean Paul Richter. When did he live?.,...292, 290

Mention five noted German scientists. Give facts about the life and writings of each.......................292, 441-497

Who was Hegel? What system of philosophy was taught by him? When did Schopenhauer live? What did he write?.444, 290

At what time did Jakob and Wilhelm Grimm live? What did they write besides "Household Tales"?.................290, 440

For what profession did Heine prepare? Mention three of his best-known works................................. 444

Name five German historians. Give facts about the lives of Neander, Niebuhr, Ranke........................292, 470-479

94

What is the character of Auerbach's writings? To what
  classes of writers do Mühlbach, Freytag, and Paul Heyse
  belong?..401, 292, 290

Mention three noted operas to which both libretto and music were
  written by Richard Wagner...........................   497

Give the name of one German writer born in the 15th century.
  One in the 16th. One in the 17th. Six in the 18th. Three
  in the 19th..289-290

Relate the story of the Pied Piper of Hamelin. What was
  Koppelberg?..375, 333

What is the German legend of the trusty Eckhardt?.......328, 354

In German tradition who was the Lorelei? What was a gnome?
  A kobold?....................................334, 330, 333

FRENCH LITERATURE

From what time do the most ancient documents of the French
  language date? What are the four divisions of the early
  literature of France?...................................   293

Is the song of Roland earlier or later than the troubadours?
  What is its theme?...........................74, 293, 378

What are the Arthurian romances? Tell the romance of the
  sangraal. Of Charlemagne.......................345, 360, 350

What was the nature of the songs of the troubadours? By
  what name were the troubadours known in northern France?
  By what names were similar singers known in Germany and
  England?...385, 76

Who was Abélard? What did he write? Give an account of
  his romantic life....................................292, 393

At what time were oriental legends brought into France? During
  what centuries were the "fabliaux" popular? What are
  they?..293, 357

In what two centuries and by what two authors was the "Romance
  of the Rose" written? Discuss the character of the poem.
  Give a brief synopsis of it. Outline the story of "Robert
  the Devil" and tell when it was written................293, 378

In what way did the crusades stimulate dramatic writing in
  France? Give an account of French drama in the 14th
  and 15th centuries.....................................   293

What document is probably the oldest French prose? Give
  its date. When were the laws of William the Conqueror
  written?...   294

Name the chroniclers of the 12th, 14th and 15th centuries. Of
  what countries is Froissart's "Chronicles" a record?........   294

By what events was the literature of France greatly influenced during the 15th century?.............................. 294

What is meant by the *renaissance?* Compare the effects of the *renaissance* in France with those in Italy and Germany... 294

Outline the characters Gargantua and Pantagruel. Name the work in which they appear. In what century was it popular? Who is the author?...........................359, 374, 294

Give an account of the life and writings of John Calvin. What tendency of the times is shown in Montaigne's writings? 415, 294, 467

Name three dramatists, two writers of fiction, four orators, and three influential patrons of learning—all of the 17th century. What prestige did the French language acquire throughout Europe at this time?.................................. 294

Mention three representative works of Corneille. On which is his fame based? Explain the origin of his character Cid Campeador...422, 350

Tell something of Molière and the purpose of his plays. In which plays do Tartufe, Sganarelle, and Agnes occur? Tell the story of the "Love Doctor"................467, 294, 343-383

What position does Racine occupy in French literature? Name some of his works. Which is sometimes called the greatest? 479, 292

In what fields are Descartes and Bossuet noted? Give some details of the life of each. To what century do they belong? 292, 426, 410

Why is the early part of the 18th century called a dead season of French literature? Name three novelists of the century. 294, 292

What is the character of Voltaire's writings? Show his versatility by mentioning some of his works. Why was he exiled from France?.......................................497, 294

How was Rousseau's early life spent? Name the most famous of his writings. What is the nature of his "Émile"?.483, 294, 355

Describe the character Gil Blas. By whom was "Gil Blas" written? Name some other works by the same author. 360, 294, 456

What is the story of "Paul and Virginia"? Tell something of the author..375, 406

Who wrote the "Barber of Seville"? Justify the term many-sided genius as applied to the writer...................295, 404

For what lyric is Rouget de Lisle famous? Compare with other French lyric poems...................................... 295

Name Montesquieu's greatest work.......................467, 294

Name two eminent naturalists of the 18th century. State some
facts about their lives...........................292, 413, 424

For what sorts of literary productions are Chateaubriand and
Madame de Staël celebrated? Name two works of each..295, 292

Give the names of five French historians of the 19th century.
Mention one work of each. Which has been called the
greatest French writer of his time?.............295, 441-494

For what are Cousin, Comte, Renan noted?.................295, 480

Give a brief sketch of the life and writings of Jules Michelet...466, 293

Mention three noted modern French dramatists............... 295

Give a brief sketch of the life of Balzac. What is the extent of
his works?...295, 403

When did Victor Hugo live? Name three of his works. Which
is his greatest production?...........................447, 295

Sketch the life of Dumas the Elder. Which of his books have
been most popular? How was Alexandre Dumas, born 1824,
related to Alexandre Dumas, born 1802?...............428, 295

What did Eugène Sue write? Compare the birth dates of Dumas
the elder and Sue................................295, 492, 428

Is George Sand a real name? What are the names of three of
her books?...295, 485

What is the character of the writings of Taine? Jules Verne?
Sardou?.......................................293, 492, 485

To what class of writers does Zola belong? Maupassant?.293, 504, 463

For what profession did Calvin prepare? Corneille? Molière?
Balzac? Thiers?...................................403-494

Give the work and the author from which each of the following is
taken: Candide, Consuelo, Le Menteur, Pantagruleon law
case, Quasimodo, Rigolette..........................349-377

What is the Gesta Romanorum?............................ 359

Give the real names of the following writers: Pierre Loti, George
Sand, Voltaire, Max O'Rell...............292-293, 322-323

ITALIAN LITERATURE

How old are some of the manuscripts preserved in Italian libraries? Name three of them. What is a palimpsest?.....309, 374

Explain how culture was kept alive in Italy during the middle
ages. Was the taste of the Italians at that time for legends
and poems or for serious history?...................... 309

What early Italian traveler and writer described Cipango? Of
what interest did Italy find his travels?.................350, 309

During what century did the real Italian literature begin? What
was the character of the literature developed?............. 309

What two religious orders influenced Italian life and letters in the 13th century? To what two writers are most of the poems and hymns attributed?........................... 309

With whom did the Italian drama begin? Show how his personal influence led to the development of the drama.........309-310

What Italian dialect became the language of literature? What was the first prose work written in Italian?................. 310

Tell some facts about Guittone d' Arezzo. Whom did he take for his model?.. 310

In what century and by whom was the "Golden Legend" written? Why is it deserving of study?........................... 360

Explain why the year 1282 is regarded as marking the period of development of Italian literature........................ 310

Describe the writings of Cavalcanti. Of what political party was he the head? Of whom was he a close friend?............. 310

Give an account of the life of Dante, with dates of birth and death. Name his principal works. How does Dante rank with other writers of his time?........................424, 310

Tell briefly of what Dante's "Vita Nuova" consists. What is the nature of his "Convito"? Of "De Monarchia"?..... 310

Outline carefully the "Divine Comedy". State to what class of poetry it belongs, into what parts it is divided, what questions it discusses................................352, 310

Why was the "Divine Comedy" so named by Dante? What effect had this poem upon Italian literature?...........310-311

What sort of poems were written by Cina de Pistoia? Give three facts about his personal and literary standing...... 311

How is Petrarch classed in histories of literature? In what other way is he equally well known? Relate in brief the events of his life....................................311, 476

When did Boccaccio live? What is his most celebrated work? Of what does it consist? Mention some other subjects on which he wrote..................................408, 352, 311

Mention a writer whose work is still consulted as an authority on Florentine history of the 12th and 13th centuries.......... 311

For what is Lorenzo de' Medici chiefly remembered? What was his influence as a scholar? Why did Savonarola oppose him? Give facts about the lives of both men. 311, 465, 485

Name two leading Italian historians. How did their studies of historical conditions differ? Mention one work by each. 311, 309, 460

When did Ariosto live? What is his greatest work?........399, 312

When and by whom was "Orlando Furioso" written? State what kind of poetry it is, its theme, its characteristics, its popularity. Who is Genevra?.................373, 399, 312, 359

Who was Torquato Tasso? Give a short account of his life. Name his greatest work. What does it describe?. .493, 309, 312

Give a synopsis of Tasso's "Jerusalem Delivered". Who were Godfrey de Bouillon, Armida, Rinaldo, Ubaldo, Clorinda, Erminia, Adrastus, Ademar?..................364, 438, 343-385

Under what rule did the period of decadence in Italian literature begin? How long did this condition last? By what name is it known?...................................... 312

In what different fields of learning was Galileo conspicuous? Name his inventions and discoveries. Give other events of his life. Characterize Galileo's prose.................312, 435

When was Italy freed from Spanish dominion? What sort of writing appeared first in this new period? By what was it followed? 312

At what time did Botta, Sismondi, and Colletta live? To what class of writers do they belong? Which wrote a history of the American revolution?...................312, 309, 410, 488

When was the movement known as romanticism prominent? Compare this with the *renaissance*. Mention the first realistic writer of Italy. State Goethe's estimate of him.312, 294

For what is Gabriele Rossetti celebrated? What position did he occupy in England? Give the names of his son and his daughter, and tell something of their literary and artistic attainments... 483

Compare Leopardi's writings with those of Shelley and Byron. Also compare dates of birth, and ages at death. .312, 456, 296-297

Name three fiction writers of the 19th century. Two political writers... 312

What position do the works of De Amicis hold? 312

Give an account of the life and writings of Gabriele d' Annunzio. 398

SPANISH LITERATURE

What is the oldest specimen of Spanish literature? The earliest important work? From what century do they date?..... 313

Who was the Cid? How has he been immortalized in fiction? 419-420, 350

What is the character of the 13th century literature of Spain? Name three writers of that century....................... 313

Who is the author of "The Philosopher's Stone"? Who was the originator of history written in Spanish? What is the "Cronica General"? During whose reign was it compiled?. 313

Trace the influence of Alfonso X through the historical literature of the 14th century............................... 313

State some facts about the writings of Juan Manuel and Pedro Lopez de Ayala...............................313, 312

In what century were the French romances of the "round table" translated and imitated in Spain?..................... 313

What is meant by the "arte de trobar"? During whose reign did it appear? Of what was it composed? Mention two writers of such verse................................. 313

How did Spanish drama begin? Trace its development. When and by whom was "La Celestina" written? What effect had it? 313

From the union of what kingdoms does the golden age of Spanish literature date?.. 314

Give a concise biography of Cervantes. What was the character of his first writings? Name an English author whose death occurred in the same year as Cervantes' death.........417, 295

What is the nature of Cervantes' "Don Quixote"? Tell something of these characters: Don Quixote, Sancho Panza, Mambrino, Camacho, Ubeda.....................353, 349-385

What did Lope de Vega write? Of whom was he a contemporary?
....314, 313

Who was the leading Spanish dramatist during the golden age? Divide his plays into four classes......................314, 414

State how the historical writings of Juan de Mariana differed from those of earlier Spanish writers. Name three Spanish historians who wrote of the new world................314, 313

To what extent are such subjects as philosophy, mathematics, etc., represented in Spanish literature?.................... 314

From what source did the 16th century poets draw much of their inspiration? To what extent has Spanish poetry influenced the national life?.. 314

Why did Spanish literature make little progress during the first half of the 18th century? What was the influence of Charles III upon literature?...................................... 314

Outline Spanish literature of the 19th century. What author wrote under the pen name Figaro? Name a famous novel of the century and its author....................... 314

RUSSIAN LITERATURE

Describe the oral traditions which were the foundation of Russian literature. By what name are they known?.............314-315

Into what five periods is the oral literature divided? What are the characteristics of the tales of the first three periods?.314-315

What are the principal themes of the tales of the fourth period, in which Moscow became the capital of Russia? Give the date of its beginning.. 315

Show how the accession of Peter the Great is marked by distinct legendary tales... 315

In what century and by whom were some of Russia's songs and folk-tales preserved in written form?..................... 315

What is the earliest specimen of written Russian literature? What is its date?... 315

Mention three prose writings of the 11th century. By whom was most of the writing of these times done?............:. 315

Who is called the patriarch of Russian literature? What are his writings?.. 315

What is the "Story of Igor"? At what time and by whom was the "Book of Household Management" written?......... 315

When was the first printing press set up in Moscow? When was the first book printed? What was this book?....... 315

Name the most important Russian writing of the first half of the 17th century. Where was it written? At that time what treatment did writers of educational works receive?......... 315

What country influenced Russia during the 17th century? With what writers did the old Russian literature end?........316, 315

In what ways did Alexis stimulate the progress of learning? What books did he burn? When did he reign?............316, 395

When did Peter the Great become czar? What was his influence in regard to the use of the Russian language?..........149, 316

Name three writers of the time of Peter the Great. State the purpose of the works of each............................ 316

What was the attitude of Catherine II toward literature? Name the greatest poet of her reign.........................417, 316

Who wrote "A Journey to Moscow"? What journey did the author make in consequence of this work?................. 316

Mention the most celebrated writer of Russian fables. Who is called the first novelist of talent? Of what did he write?. 316

Explain what is meant by Little Russia. When was all publication in the language of Little Russia forbidden? Who was the poet of Little Russia? What name is given to the cairn marking his grave?...................................... 317

What class of people form the main subject of Turgenieff's works? Give an estimate of the author. Of his "Nest of Gentle People"..316, 495

Give dates of birth and death of Tolstoi. Name four of his works. Which do critics consider his best works?.......495, 316

Name three Russian historians of the 19th century. Which is called the ablest of his time?............................ 317

State the subject of Count Witte's writings. What important positions were held by him?............................ 503

What is the real name of Maxim Gorky? Give a brief review of his life and writings....................................... 439

JAPANESE LITERATURE

From what century does Japanese literature date? How early are historical compilations said to have existed?......... 317

Give the title of the earliest known Japanese writing. Explain fully how it was compiled.............................. 317

What is the most ancient poem in Japanese literature? To what century does it belong?........................... 317

Name a Japanese history completed in 720. Compare this with the "Kojiki". In these ancient histories what name is given to Japan?... 317

What is the "Tosa Nikki"? In what century and by whom was it written?... 318

During the 10th century what place did women occupy in Japanese literature?..................................... 318

By whom and in what century was the "Dai Nihonshi" composed? What was its purpose? Why have the national annals of Japan been so carefully guarded?............. 317

What do the Japanese works on geography cover?........... 318

Describe the poetry of Japan. Mention two poetic forms that do not appear in Japanese literature..................... 318

What sorts of fiction are common in the literature of Japan?... 318

Mention a reference work of great value to students of Japanese language and literature....................................318

ENGLISH LITERATURE

Name the oldest song of the Northmen which has been preserved in English literature....................................... 297

How old is "Beowulf"? Outline it briefly. To what class of poetry does it belong?............................295, 347, 297

What is the first great native British poem?.................298, 295

Under what influence did literature begin in England? In what century and in what part of the country? For how many centuries was learning confined to this locality?............ 297

Who was the first writer of English prose? What did he write? State the extent of his fame...........................298, 295

Trace the development of literature in the 9th century. Give dates and effect of Danish invasions and conquest. What place is called the cradle of English poetry? The home of English prose?....................................298, 69-70

To what extent and in what way did Alfred the Great advance English language and literature?...................298, 295, 395

When did Ælfric write? What is the best model of English at the beginning of the 11th century?....................295, 298

Why was the Norman conquest so important an event in literature? What was its effect?......................72, 298

Describe the literature of England during the 12th century. What did Geoffrey of Monmouth write?.................... 298

Give the four cycles into which 12th and 13th century romance is divided. Tell some of the traditions of King Arthur, Arthur's drinking-horn, Arthur's round table, the graal, Sir Tristram, Roland, Charlemagne, Robin Hood........298, 345-385

When were the first dramas produced in England? On what are the mysteries and miracle-plays founded? Give date and name of the earliest miracle-play on record........299, 371

Mention Roger Bacon's greatest work. Who was he? To what century does he belong?.............................402, 295

Name two prose writers of the 14th century, mentioning one work of each. Who wrote "Piers Plowman"? What is it?....298, 375

Give a brief account of the life and writings of Chaucer. What is his greatest work? In what dialect did he write?.419, 298-299

State the theme of the Canterbury tales. What is the literary value of the prologue?...........................350, 298-299

What connection has each of the following with the Canterbury tales: Tabard inn, Harry Baillie, Arcite, Donegild, Griselda, Valerian, the pardoner's tale, Madame Eglantine? From what sources does Chaucer derive some of his tales?....345-385

Summarize the literary events of the 14th century. Name the greatest writer? Whose name stands second?...........299, 298

Characterize 15th century English literature. What was the greatest prose work of the century? When and by whom was the first book printed in England? What was it?.......299, 417

Of what nature is Malory's "Morte d' Arthur"? Tell something of the author..299, 461

Name Sir Thomas More's most celebrated work. Give a short outline of it.....................................295, 468, 385

Who made the first complete English translation of the scriptures? The second? When and by whom was the first copy of the whole Bible printed?...........................298, 299

What is meant by the golden age in English literature? What conditions stimulated intellectual activity at this time?... 299

What rank does Spenser take among writers of the Elizabethan age? Mention two of his works........................ 299

Describe Spenser's "Shepherd's Calendar".................299, 381

Outline the "Faerie Queene". Tell something of interest about
each of the following: Red-cross knight, Una, Acrasia, Guyon,
Archimago, Duessa, Canace, Serena, Calidore, the blatant
beast, Florimel, Malengrin, Philtra, Ignaro..........357, 343-385

Name some dramas by Christopher Marlowe. In what year was
he born? Compare date of his birth with the birth date of
Shakespere..299, 295

Tell what is known of the life of Shakespere. Name three of his
contemporaries. How many plays did he write?........487, 299

Name three of Shakespere's tragedies. Three of his comedies.
Estimate the literary value of his works..............487, 299

Tell the story of—"As You Like It", "Twelfth Night", "Othello",
"King Lear", "Winter's Tale"........................346-386

Describe each of the following characters and tell in which of
Shakespere's plays each occurs: Banquo, Bardolph, Bene-
dick, Caliban, Falstaff, Jaques, Queen Mab, Nick Bottom,
Prospero, Romeo, Shylock, Timon, Viola...............346-386

What is considered the measure of Shakespere's literary greatness? In what way does he excel other writers?........299-300

Mention three dramas produced by Ben Jonson. How was his
early life spent? Contrast Jonson's delineation of character
with that of Shakespere. What is the nature of "Every Man
in His Humor"?...............................300, 452, 356

When did the decay of English drama begin? How do the plays of
Fletcher and Beaumont compare with those of Shakespere?..300, 433

Who was the greatest prose writer of the Elizabethan age? In
what three fields of literature was he prominent? Give a
sketch of his life...................................300, 402

Name and describe Bacon's greatest work. When was it published? In what language? What is his "New Atlantis"?.300, 372

What name is given to the literary period following the Elizabethan? Contrast its characteristics with those of the
Elizabethan age. Were its writings chiefly prose or poetry?. 300

In what year was the King James version of the Bible printed?
What was its effect upon the speech of the people?......... 300

What place does Milton occupy among English writers? Describe
his boyhood, his education, his later life................300, 466

Mention five of Milton's early poems. Tell something of each.
Which of these is considered his finest poem?........... 300

To what class of writing was Milton devoted from 1640 to 1660?
Give the name of his greatest prose work. Who were the
rulers of England during that time?....................301, 151

Describe briefly "Paradise Lost". What is its style? To what
classic writers may Milton be compared?................. 301
Who is called the second greatest writer of the puritan age? State
the comparative standing of Shakespere, Milton, Bunyan.. 301
Give the principal facts regarding the life of John Bunyan. With
what idea was "Pilgrim's Progress" written?........413, 301, 376
Outline the story of "Pilgrim's Progress". Who are Christian,
Hopeful, giant Despair? What are doubting castle, the
slough of despond, and the valley of humiliation?..376, 350-385
Tell something of Samuel Pepys's "Diary". How was it written?.301, 375
What is the great historical work of the puritan age? Of whom
was its author an exact contemporary?................... 301
Contrast Dryden's poetry with that of Chaucer and Spenser.
Name three of his poems. When did Dryden live?...301, 299, 428
Compare Dryden's literary style with that of Pope. What influ-
ence had their writings upon English speech?............301-302
Describe the conditions of Pope's time. Give a sketch of his life.
Name two of his poems. Which of the classics did he trans-
late?...301-302, 478
Name the greatest work of John Locke. Of Sir Isaac Newton.
State some facts about each......................296, 458, 470
For what sort of writing is the first half of the 18th century
notable? What writers developed a new style of essays?... 302
What was the "Tatler"? The "Spectator"? The "Guardian"?
By whom were they published? Name some contributors.
What is the value of Addison's essays? Tell something of
his life..302, 382, 394
At what time did prose fiction develop in England? Who was
the first fiction writer of the century?................... 302
What are Daniel Defoe's best-known works? Tell the story of
"Robinson Crusoe"..............................302, 426, 378
Who wrote "Gulliver's Travels"? The "Tale of a Tub"? Give
a short sketch of the author's life. What is the character
of "Gulliver's Travels"? What is Lilliput land? Laputa?
....302, 492, 361-367
Mention two novels by Fielding. Name two by Richardson.
Smollett. Sterne. Tell something of each work....302, 344-381
Give some facts about Fielding, Smollett, Sterne. Which is
called the father of English fiction?...................433-490
How does the "Vicar of Wakefield" rank among novels of the
18th century? Outline the life of Goldsmith. Give the
theme of the "Vicar of Wakefield", "She Stoops to Conquer", "The Deserted Village"................302, 438, 352-386

Mention well-known poems by Gray, Collins, Cowper. What is
the literary value of Gray's work?..............302, 296, 439

Name three 18th century historians. Two distinguished orators.
Tell something of their lives and their literary standing.
What did Blackstone write?....................302, 407-448

Give an account of the literary work carried on by Dr. Samuel
Johnson. What is his most famous work? Why did he
write "Rasselas"? Who was Boswell?........302, 451, 377, 410

What are the themes of Burns's poems? Give the titles of three
poems. At what age did Burns die?..........302, 296, 413-414

Name the English poets of the early part of the 19th century.
What changes are observed in the poetry of this time?
....302-303

What was the aim of Wordsworth's poetry? Name one of his
best poems. Quote the first lines of three.........303, 389-390

What is meant by poet laureate? Name the first poet laureate.
The present one. Mention four laureates of the 19th century. When did Wordsworth become poet laureate?...365-366, 503

Name Coleridge's finest poems. Mention some poems by Shelley.
By Keats. Who was the ancient mariner? Endymion?
....303, 297, 344, 355

Of what nationality was Thomas Moore? What is his best-
known work? What is the "Loves of the Angels"? Explain
the following allusions: Nourmahal, Nucta, the veiled
prophet.....................................303, 296, 368-386

For what is Byron's poetry remarkable? After the production
of which poem was it that Byron "awoke one morning and
found himself famous"? What is the plan of "Childe
Harold"? Of "Manfred"?...................303, 414, 350, 370

Sketch the lives of Byron, Shelley, Keats. State the parentage
of each and the age of each at death....................414-487

Mention five prose writers of the first half of the 19th century.
In what fields of literature were they prominent? Which
will be remembered as the creator of the historical novel? 303

Give a brief outline of the life of Sir Walter Scott. Name three
of his poems. What are the Waverley novels? Who are
the following characters : Dandie Dinmont, Ivanhoe, lady
of the lake, Lochinvar, Red-gauntlet?........486, 386, 351-377

Of what class were most of the writings of Lamb, De Quincey,
Macaulay, John Stuart Mill? State some item of interest
from the life of each..........................303, 426-466

In what year did the Victorian age of English literature begin?
For what is it chiefly known?........................... 303

Name two poets, two writers of prose fiction, two essayists, two philosophers, and two historians of the Victorian age..... 303

Give the title of one poem by Robert Browning. One by Elizabeth Barrett Browning. In what countries did they spend many years? Tell something of the "Ring and the Book", the Pied Piper of Hamelin", "Pippa Passes"......297, 412, 375-378

In what year was Tennyson born? What honors were conferred upon him in 1850 and in 1884? What is the purpose of the "Idylls of the King"?...............................493, 363

To what extent do the old legends of King Arthur enter into the "Idylls of the King"? Who was Elaine? Sir Galahad? 345-359

Is Matthew Arnold's reputation based chiefly upon his work as an author or as a critic? What educational positions did he hold? Mention two of his works.....................400, 297

What place does Bulwer-Lytton occupy in English fiction? Describe his brilliant literary career. Give the titles of his two best-known works...............................460, 297

Which class of people furnished material for Thackeray's novels? For Dickens's? For George Eliot's?...................... 303

Give a sketch of the life of Thackeray. What did he study in Paris? Name four of his books. Describe these characters: Col. Newcome, Mr. Sedley, Becky Sharp...........494, 372-381

Describe the hardships of Dickens's early life. Sketch his later successes. What did Dickens purpose to accomplish in most of his novels?.......................................427, 303

Describe each of the following characters. State in which of Dickens's novels each occurs: Sydney Carton, Mrs. Gamp, Gradgrind, Uriah Heep, Mrs. Jellyby, Mrs. Nickleby, Scrooge, Bill Sikes...349-382

Give the real name of George Eliot. Name her best works. Give the first line of "The Choir Invisible"..........430, 297, 388

What lesson did Carlyle undertake to teach? Compare the teachings of Carlyle and Ruskin. Give dates of birth and some details of the life of each. Name two of Carlyle's books. Two of Ruskin's........................303, 416, 484

In what line of writing is Herbert Spencer prominent? What was his early occupation?..................................303, 489

Of what did the following write: Hugh Miller, Darwin, Tyndall, Huxley? In what century did they live? What was the effect of Darwin's work?..........................297, 425-496

What histories were written by Grote, Rawlinson, Froude, Green?...297, 435-479

What was the purpose of Charles Reade's novels? Name three of them..479, 297

Give the names of three works by Charles Kingsley. State the character of each. What was Kingsley's profession?..453, 297

Mention one work by Anthony Trollope. State something of his life..297, 495

Sketch briefly the life of Charlotte Bronté. Mention three of her books. What was the success of "Jane Eyre"? How does it rank?.......................................411, 297

For what profession did Thomas Hughes prepare? Name some of his principal works..............................447, 297

Mention some writings by George Meredith. Where was he educated?... 465

Tell something of Richard Blackmore and his works......407, 297

What positions were occupied by Sir Edwin Arnold? Name his most important work...........................400, 297

In what year was James Bryce born? Mention some of the important offices held by him. Name three of his books..297, 412

Give the names of two poems by Swinburne. Mention an essay and a play by Swinburne............................... 492

Name two books by John Watson. Under what pseudonym did he write? What was his profession in early life?..... 498

Give the names of three works by Hall Caine. When and where was he born? What was his early profession?............ 414

State the nationality of James M. Barrie. Mention four of his works for the stage. Give the titles of his first four books... 403

Tell something of the life of Robert Louis Stevenson. Name four of his books. Where did he spend his last years?..... 490

Sketch briefly the life of Henry Rider Haggard. Name two of his best-known works................................ 441

Where was Rudyard Kipling born? Mention five of his works. Quote the first line of the "Recessional"................453, 390

What English poet is called the poet's poet? The father of English poetry? The bard of Avon? The bard of Rydal Mount? 299, 298, 346

What is the real name of each of the following English writers: Currer Bell, Marie Corelli, Boz, Ian MacLaren, Gavin Ogilvy, Lewis Carroll?...............................321-323

Name the author of each of the following: "Lorna Doone", "Vanity Fair", "The Woman in White", "Jane Eyre", "Scottish Chiefs", "The Compleat Angler", "Last Days of Pompeii", "Pride and Prejudice"......................296-297

Identify the following characters in stories, plays, or poems, and
  name the author: John Barleycorn, Captain Bobadil, Doctor
  Jekyll and Mr. Hyde, Dolly Varden, Fagin, Tam O'Shanter,
  Tommy Atkins.................................346-384
Name the authors of the following poems: "Crossing the Bar",
  "The Cotter's Saturday Night", "Lucile", "The Lost Chord",
  "Lays of Ancient Rome"......................388-389, 296-297
Give the title and the author of each of the poems beginning with
  the following lines:
  "A thing of beauty is a joy forever."
  "Flow gently, sweet Afton, among thy green braes."
  "How does the water come down at Lodore?"
  "Sweet and low, sweet and low."
  "Lead, kindly light, amid the encircling gloom."
  "The year's at the spring."
  "Drink to me only with thine eyes."...................387-390

AMERICAN LITERATURE

Why are American history and American literature not contem-
  poraneous terms?....................................... 306
Mention three periods into which American literature is divided.
  What years are included in each of the three periods?...... 306
Why did the character of colonial literature vary in different
  parts of the country?.................................. 306
Give a brief description of the literature of Virginia during the
  colonial period. Who is the author of "A True Relation of
  Virginia"? When and where was it published?.......... 306
Mention two narratives and descriptions of the new world, pub-
  lished in the 17th century. By whom and for what purpose
  were they written?..................................... 306
Compare the progress of education in New England with that of
  Virginia during the colonial period. What was the first
  book printed in the New England colonies?.............. 306
State the nature of the earliest writings in New England. In
  what form were the events of the first year of the Plymouth
  colony recorded?....................................... 306
Who wrote the "History of Plymouth"? To what date does it
  extend?... 306
What was the character of the literature of New England throughout the colonial period? Explain...................... 306
Mention six writers of the colonial period. Which three of these
  were the greatest?..........................304, 306, 307
What is the representative work of John Winthrop? What
  position did he hold?.............................304, 503

Mention three facts concerning the life of Cotton Mather. What is the nature of the "Magnalia"?...............463, 307, 369

Give a concise biography of Jonathan Edwards and mention three of his works. Which is best known?.............430, 307

Name three representative works of Benjamin Franklin. Give a short account of his life. What did "Poor Richard's Almanac" contain?.............................307, 434, 376

In what year was the first newspaper published in America? Give the name and the date of the second. The third.......... 307

What was the character of the writings of the revolutionary period? What literary value have its state papers?........ 307

Who was the greatest orator of Massachusetts during the revolutionary period? Of Virginia? Mention five statesmen of the revolutionary period who were able writers. Name some of the state papers partly produced by Thomas Jefferson..307, 450

Tell the origin of "Yankee Doodle"......................... 307

Who is the author of the "Battle of the Kegs"?................ 304

Where was the literary center of America during the early part of the 19th century?..................................... 307

What is the representative work of Noah Webster? Name three other works. Tell something of his life...............304, 499

Who are the best-known writers of the first half of the 19th century? Name three prose writers and three poets of that century..307-308

Divide the New England writers of the 19th century into three groups. Mention three prominent names from each group.307-308

Give the names of the great orators of the North. With what orators of the South were these contemporaneous?........ 308

In what century were the following born: Daniel Webster, Edward Everett, Rufus Choate, Henry Clay, Robert Hayne, John C. Calhoun? Name Webster's most brilliant address. What did Everett write? What rank has Choate as an orator?.....414-499

Mention two works by William Ellery Channing. How does his literary style compare with that of other American writers?. 418

Tell something of the writings of Joseph Story and Thomas Hart Benton...304, 491, 405

Give a concise biography of Washington Irving. For what profession was Irving prepared? Name six of his writings. Associate one of his books with his life in Spain......... 448

Tell the story of Rip Van Winkle. In what work does it occur? Who was Diedrich Knickerbocker? To what was the name Salmagundi applied?...........................378, 364, 379

What well-known American authors were born during the American revolution?.......................................139, 304

Give a brief sketch of the life of James Fenimore Cooper. Into what languages have Cooper's works been translated?..... 422

On what historical fact is Cooper's "Pilot" based? Name the books composing the "Leather-Stocking Tales". Outline the story running through the series. As what character does Natty Bumppo appear in the different tales?......376, 366, 371

Give the first lines of "The American Flag" and "The Culprit Fay". Who wrote them? When did he live?.......387-388, 304

Mention one poem by Fitz-Greene Halleck. Quote its first line..304, 389

Give a biographical sketch of William Cullen Bryant. At what age was "Thanatopsis" written? Name some of his other writings. Give the first line of the "Death of the Flowers". Of "To a Waterfowl". Of "Thanatopsis".........412, 388-390

By whom were "Hail, Columbia", "The Star-Spangled Banner", "Home, Sweet Home", "America" written? State facts about the authors. During what war was "The Star-Spangled Banner" written?....................304-305, 447-475

What is the representative work of Joseph E. Worcester? When was it published?....................................304, 503

When and where was Ralph Waldo Emerson born? How does he rank among American writers? Mention three representative works of Emerson. Of what English philosopher was Emerson a friend? Which of the two was older?..431, 297

State the topics of Emerson's "Representative Men". Quote the first line of the "Concord Hymn".....................377, 388

Mention four of the representative works of Nathaniel Hawthorne. Upon which does his reputation mainly rest? Outline the plot of the "Scarlet Letter"..............304, 444, 380

Where was Brook Farm? What literary people were connected with it? In which of Hawthorne's romances is the story told? 348

Relate the principal events in the life of Longfellow. What was his education? Mention four of his most celebrated poems. Name another American poet born in the same year......458, 305

From what source did Longfellow gather the material for "Hiawatha"? Who was Minnehaha? Osseo?................362-373

What is the subject of Longfellow's "Evangeline"? Name its principal characters. In what poem do Miles Standish and Priscilla appear? What are the "Tales of a Wayside Inn"?..356-383

Where was John G. Whittier born? Of what descent was he? What trade did he learn? At what time was he a member of the legislature?...................................... 501

Name three of Whittier's poems. Quote the first line of the "Barefoot Boy". Of "Maud Muller"..............501, 387, 389

For what works is Oliver Wendell Holmes best known? In what magazine did they first appear? Quote the first lines of "The Boys", "The Chambered Nautilus", and "The Last Leaf".

....446, 388-389

Tell something of the life of Edgar Allan Poe. How do his writings compare with those of other American poets?....477, 307

Give the first lines of "Annabel Lee" and "The Raven". By whom were they written? Where is the scene of "The Gold Bug" laid?.....................................387, 390, 360

By what address did Abraham Lincoln attain fame as an orator? In what year were Lincoln, Holmes, and Poe born?..308, 457, 305

Give a brief account of the life and the writings of James Russell Lowell...459

Name in chronological order five American historians born between 1795 and 1825...................................304-305, 308

Of what countries did Prescott write history? Mention two historical works by Bancroft. What period of American history is covered by Bancroft's work? By Hildreth's? On what works is Motley's fame based? Name Parkman's best-known histories.....................................304-305, 403-478

What government positions were held by Motley? How did Parkman gather material for "The Conspiracy of Pontiac"?..469, 474

In what circumstances was Thoreau's "Walden" written? Of what is it a record? To what department of science was Thoreau devoted? Of whom was he a friend?..........494, 386

What are five representative works of Harriet Beecher Stowe? Which one is most famous? Tell something of her life.....491

For what poem is Julia Ward Howe best known? Where was it written? Quote its first line.........................447, 387

Sketch briefly the life of Edward Everett Hale. Mention five well-known works. "Ten Times One Is Ten" led to the founding of what society?.....................................441, 383

Outline the army service of Lew Wallace. Name four of his books. Give a synopsis of "Ben Hur"...............497, 347

Name three humorous writers of the 19th century. Which of them wrote both prose and poetry?................308, 305, 306

Where was Samuel L. Clemens born? Sketch his early life. Under what name did he write? Mention five of his works. Outline briefly the character Tom Sawyer.............420, 384

What state was the birthplace of William Dean Howells? What position did he occupy at Venice? Name an American magazine edited by him. Give the titles of three of his best novels. What material furnishes themes for much of his work?....447, 308

To what class of writers does Thomas Bailey Aldrich belong? Sketch his life. What magazine did he edit? Name two of his poems and one prose work........................395, 305

Outline the life of Edmund Clarence Stedman. Mention three of his works. To what class of critics does he belong?.490, 305, 308

Quote the first line of a poem by John Burroughs. On what subject are most of Burroughs's works? Name three of his books. Give some facts about his early life.........390, 414

Who was Thomas Wentworth Higginson? What did he write?.446, 305

Give the name of one work by George W. Curtis. One by Charles Dudley Warner. One by Frank R. Stockton..... 305

In what different occupations did Bret Harte engage? Name two of his writings...................................... 443

Who wrote "Ramona"? Why is it especially noteworthy? Name the best writers on the American Indian besides the author of the leather-stocking tales...........................377, 366

What is the character of Eugene Field's poems? What is he sometimes called? Sketch his early life. Give the title and the first line of one of his poems...................433, 389

Why is James Whitcomb Riley called the Hoosier poet? What was his early education? Mention five of his poems. Give the first lines of "Out to Old Aunt Mary's" and "Knee-deep in June". 481, 389

Outline the life of Henry James. Name two of his works....449, 305

Name two southern poets, and five fiction writers of southern birth. 308

What rare qualities did Sidney Lanier possess? Give the title of one prose work. With what words does the "Song of the Chattahoochee" begin? Sketch his life............308, 390, 455

Who wrote "When Malindy Sings"? Quote its first line. Estimate the literary value of Paul Laurence Dunbar's poems. 390, 308

Tell something of the career of George W. Cable. Name three of his books...414, 305

Where was Thomas Nelson Page born? State his education. What diplomatic appointment did he receive in 1913? Name three of his books...................................... 473

Sketch the life of James Lane Allen. In what colleges did he teach? What are the titles of five of his books?.......... 396

In what state was Joel Chandler Harris born? To what trade was he apprenticed? Tell something of the character of his writings as judged from their titles................. 443

Under what name did Mary N. Murfree for years conceal her identity? Mention some of her books................... 469

For what profession did Thomas Dixon, jr., prepare? Give the titles of two of his writings.............................. 428

Give an account of the life of Henry Van Dyke. What has he
written? What diplomatic post did he accept in 1913?..... 496
Give the names of three works of fiction by Richard Harding
Davis. In what wars did he serve as a correspondent?...... 425
Mention some works of fiction by Margaretta Wade Deland. By
Ellen Glasgow..426, 438
Mention five books by Kate Douglas Wiggin. In what philan-
thropic work has she been interested?................... 501
Name a work on history by Woodrow Wilson. One on litera-
ture. One on politics...............................502-503
Give the names of two historical works by Theodore Roosevelt.
One biographical work. Two pertaining to western life... 482
State important facts about Elbert Hubbard. Give the titles
of five of his works.................................... 447
What was Owen Wister's education? His profession? What are
the titles of two well-known works by Wister?............. 503
Give a brief account of the literary, editorial, and educational
work of Bliss Perry.................................... 476
Name the American magazines edited by each of the following,
and tell something of the editor: Albert Shaw, Edward
W. Bok, George Horace Lorimer, Norman Hapgood......408-487
Mention some of the best-known books by Gene Stratton-Porter.
Give a brief account of the author's life.................. 478
What works have made Harold Bell Wright known? In what
occupations has he engaged?........................... 504
Who wrote the following: "The Hoosier Schoolmaster", "Huckle-
berry Finn", "The Lady or the Tiger", "Little Women",
"The Man without a Country", "The Oregon Trail", "Dream
Life", "Timothy Titcomb's Letters", "The Marble Faun",
"Ferdinand and Isabella", "Potiphar Papers", "The Fair
God"?..304-306
In what works do the following characters occur: Ichabod Crane,
Topsy, Alice Roussillon, Sam Slick, Tirzah, Zenobia?.....351-387
Name the author of each of these: "America", "Barbara
Frietchie", "Old Ironsides", "The Old Oaken Bucket",
"Old Folks at Home", "Songs of the Sierras", "The Vision
of Sir Launfal"...........................387-390, 382, 305
Who wrote the "Battle Hymn of the Republic"? "Leaves of
Grass"? "Lincoln"? "The Piper"?.....................305-306
Give the real names of these writers: Ralph Connor, Charles
Egbert Craddock, Martin Dooley, Fra Elbertus, Marion
Harland, Alice Caldwell Hegan, H. H., Josiah Allen's Wife, Ik
Marvel, Mark Twain, Artemus Ward, John Strange Winter. 321-323

114

GEOGRAPHY

What is the distance of the sun from the earth?.............. 725

Define latitude. Longitude...............................539, 540

Compare the size of the moon with the size of the earth. How
far away is the moon? In how long a time does the moon
make a complete revolution?............................ 717

What are tides? How many times does the tide rise and fall
each twenty-four hours? Define flood tide. Ebb tide.....574-575

Explain fully the cause of tides. When do spring tides occur?
Neap tides?..574-575

What is wind? What causes it?........................... 580

Explain the formation of dew. Why no dew on a cloudy night... 709

Of what are clouds composed? How does a fog differ from a
cloud? What is the average height of clouds?............ 696

Divide clouds into four classes and describe each class. Which
of these is highest? Which is called the rain-cloud?......696-697

Give the scientific name for "mackerel sky".................. 697

What is rain? How is it caused? Upon what does the quantity
of rainfall depend? Give in inches the mean annual deposit
of rain and dew upon the surface of the earth.............. 562

How much water is it computed that the entire atmosphere
can hold in solution? What causes the difference between
rain and snow?.. 562

What region of the world receives the greatest annual rainfall?
State in inches the greatest recorded yearly and the greatest
recorded daily precipitation. Compare this excessive rainfall
with the amount received in the interior deserts of Asia.. 515

Show the varieties of climate by comparing the tropical, arid,
and arctic regions of Asia. Where is it hottest? Where
coldest?... 515

Describe the rainbow. To what is its formation due? Where
must the observer stand in order to see a rainbow?........ 562

By what other names is the aurora borealis known? Describe
its appearance. Where is it visible? When most frequent? 688

What deceptive appearance does mirage give to distant objects?
Name localities in which it is a common occurrence........ 544

Arrange in order of size the following continents: Africa, North
America, South America, Asia, Europe, Oceania........... 852

How much of the world's surface does the Pacific ocean cover?.. 552

Through whom did Europe first learn of the Pacific? What European first saw it? Who first sailed upon it? Who takes first rank as an explorer of the Pacific?...........552, 422

Give the area and the boundaries of the Atlantic ocean. Where do the trade winds blow?.............................. 516

Describe the Gulf Stream. To what is it due? What effect has it on the climate of lands along its course?............. 536

State five facts concerning the Indian ocean................ 538

What is the southern boundary of the Arctic ocean?........ 514

What countries are separated by Bering strait? What waters does it connect? For whom was Bering strait named?..... 518

Give the names of the first five explorers who attempted to reach the north pole. Mention three of the 19th century....... 514

How far north did Nansen go? Give some facts about him. What latitude was reached by Abruzzi? For what other explorations is he celebrated?....................514, 469, 393

By whom and when was the north pole reached? Give a short biography of Robert E. Peary.....................514, 475

Mention five facts concerning 20th century Antarctic explorations. By whom was the south pole first reached? In what ship did he make the voyage?....................509, 397

Give an account of the Antarctic expedition of Captain Robert Scott. On what date did he reach the pole?.............. 509

NORTH AMERICA

What is the area of North America? Compare the areas of Canada, the United States and Mexico................ 852, 604

Where is the Rocky mountain system?....................... 565

Name the highest Rocky mountain peak in the United States. The two highest in Canada. The highest in Mexico. In Alaska. Which is the highest in North America?.......... 547

Name three principal river systems of Canada................. 522

How large a portion of the United States is drained by the Mississippi river? How long is it? What is its chief tributary? State the area of its delta.................... 544

In what state does the Missouri rise? How far is the Missouri navigable? Give the total length of the Missouri and the Mississippi...544-545

Explain the meaning of the word Mississippi. From what did the Missouri river derive its name?...................... 829

What is the name of the St. Lawrence river at its source? What lakes does it drain. State its width. Its length........570, 565

Mention three Canadian tributaries of the St. Lawrence river.... 570

Describe Lake Superior. How much higher than the Atlantic ocean is it? By what river and falls does Lake Superior flow into Lakes Huron and Michigan?...................... 573

How long is St. Mary's river? Where and what is Sault Ste. Marie? How do steamers pass these falls?............573, 839

How many islands does Lake Huron contain? How many feet above ocean level is Lake Michigan? Lake Huron?...537, 543, 539

Between what countries does Lake Erie lie? Compare the surface level of Lake Erie and Lake Ontario.............530, 539

Give a brief description of Niagara river and Niagara falls...... 549

Why was Lake Erie so named? Lake Ontario? What is the meaning of the word Niagara?......................814-832

Between what two countries does Lake Ontario form part of the boundary? Name five ports........................550-551

How do vessels pass from Lake Erie to Lake Ontario?......... 654

Which of the Great Lakes is wholly within the United States? Which is the largest? The smallest? The deepest?...543, 539

Why was the Yukon river so named? Compare it with the Mississippi in regard to length........................581, 565

Into what ocean does the Columbia river empty? How far is it navigable? For what is it famous?...................... 526

How many states compose the United States of America? Name the capital of the United States. The metropolis....624, 605, 549

What is the travel distance from Portland, Maine, to San Francisco? From New Orleans to Minneapolis?............... 863

Name the territories and the insular possessions of the United States. Describe the Virgin Islands................624-625, 577

What state in the Union has the largest area? The greatest population?...624-625

What two rivers unite to form the Ohio? How long is it? To what city is it navigable? Between what states does it form a boundary line?...................................... 550

What is the capital of the state in which you live? The area? State the origin and the meaning of its name.......626-631, 624

Give the area of New York state. Is Pennsylvania larger or smaller than New York?................................ 624

For what is the city of New York especially noted? How does it rank in size with the other cities of the world? In commerce? 549

What boroughs compose Greater New York? Mention at least six points of interest in the city of New York............. 549

Describe the Brooklyn bridge. When was it built? Give some facts about the statue of Liberty in New York harbor.779, 539

Where is Hell Gate? Why was it so named?................. 536

117

Locate the Palisades and briefly describe them. What are the highlands of the Hudson?..............................833, 820

Where is the world's greatest railway terminal? Describe it..... 533

What is Wall street? How long is Broadway, New York city? Describe Central park, New York city..............846, 549, 806

Between what two cities does the Erie canal extend? What is its length? What is meant by the term barge canal?..... 530

Where is Buffalo? What fort is located at Buffalo? What are Buffalo's principal industries?...................... 521

Where is Chautauqua lake?.................................. 807

Locate Pittsburg. Name its most important buildings. Its two chief industries. Why is it called the iron city?...... 558

How far from New York is Philadelphia?.................556-557

State some facts about Fairmount park, Philadelphia. About Independence hall. Describe the city hall. How does Philadelphia rank as a manufacturing city?............556-557

Describe briefly the city of Boston. What are some of the most important points of interest in the city?............ 519

Mention some statues and monuments of historic interest in Boston. Describe Faneuil hall. Locate Beacon Hill...519, 531, 802

How far from Boston was the battle of Lexington fought? Where is Bunker Hill monument?............................127, 519

What is the most valuable agricultural product of New York state? Massachusetts? Pennsylvania?.................648-649

Describe the site of Washington. For what purpose was it laid out? Name the principal street..................578, 834

Give a brief description of the capitol at Washington......... 578

Mention seven important government buildings in Washington. Ten noted monuments...................................578-579

Where is the Washington monument located? For what purpose was it erected? State its dimensions................ 579

How does Baltimore rank as a manufacturing and commercial city? 517

Where and what is Hampton Roads? Why is it famous?...... 818

Give the origin of the following names: Atlanta, Key West, Mount Vernon, Wheeling, Wilkesbarre................800-847

Why is Cleveland called the forest city? How does it rank with other cities of Ohio in regard to population?.......... 526

For what is Indianapolis noted?............................. 538

Locate Chicago. State the area of its public parks. Mention its principal industries.................................. 524

What city of the United States ranks first in commerce? Second?.549, 524

Name the principal public buildings and points of interest in Detroit. By whom was it founded?...................529, 133

Compare the population of Buffalo, Cleveland, and Detroit.
Show the percentage of increase between 1900 and 1910.. 582
How does St. Louis rank as a manufacturing city? As a
commercial city? Name some points of interest........570-571
In what manufacture does Minneapolis lead all other cities?.. 544
Name the most important farm product of each of these states:
Iowa, Illinois, Minnesota, North Dakota...............648-649
Give the popular names of the following states: Massachusetts,
New Hampshire, Vermont, Pennsylvania, New York..850-851
From what did Buffalo get its name? How did the names
of Chicago, Cleveland, Cincinnati, and Detroit originate?.804-811
Locate and describe the Mammoth cave...................... 541
Into what quarters is New Orleans divided? How is it protected
from the waters of the Mississippi?.....................548-549
What state is known as the Hoosier state? The blue-grass
state? The buckeye state? The lone star state? The
panhandle state?.....................................850-851
Where is the garden of the gods? Why is it so named?........ 816
Locate Denver. What is its altitude? Its climate?........... 529
Where is Pike's peak? For whom was it named? Give its
height. How is the summit reached?...................557-558
Where is the Grand canyon? Give four facts about it......... 533
Describe Yellowstone park. By whom is it owned?......580-581, 555
Locate and give history of Salt Lake City. Mention its chief
features... 568
What is the most valuable product of Nevada? Colorado? Cali-
fornia? Name the chief copper producing states......648-649, 658
Give the location, commercial importance, and industries of
Seattle. Describe its shipping facilities................... 569
Where is Spokane situated? Of what is it the center?......... 570
Describe the situation of Portland, Oregon................... 559
Where is the Yosemite valley? Give a brief description of it...581, 555
State some facts of interest about San Francisco, mentioning its
commercial rank, its harbor, its streets, its parks........... 568
State the travel distance from San Francisco to Chicago. To
New York. To Washington............................. 863
Where is Los Angeles? Name its seaport..................... 540
How is Oakland connected with San Francisco? Of what rail-
roads is it the western terminus?....................... 550
Name in order of size the ten largest cities in the United States. 582
What city in the United States is frequently referred to as Gotham?
The city of the golden gate? The city of spindles? The
monumental city? The crescent city?..................817, 783

119

Which of the United States leads in the production of corn? Spring wheat? Hay? Potatoes? Wool?...............648-649

What is the travel distance from New York to Chicago? To St. Louis? To Denver?............................... 863

Name four of the largest canals in the United States, and mention the cities connected by them...................... 653

Mention two states in which oranges are extensively grown. Which state excels in the production of rice?..........754, 648

Name the metropolis of each of the following states: New York, Pennsylvania, Illinois, Massachusetts, Missouri.....624-625

Name five of the leading cotton producing states and three of the leading gold and silver producing states............648-649

Mention three states in which coal is mined. Four in which abundant supplies of petroleum are found...........655-656, 757

Where is the present center of population of the United States? How far west has it moved in the past fifty years?....781-782

Give the boundaries of Alaska. Its capital. The principal industry. Tell something of the mining industries...... 508

Locate Mt. McKinley. How does the height of Mt. McKinley compare with other mountains of the United States?... 547

Mention the provinces of the Dominion of Canada. The capital. The metropolis......................................521, 605, 546

What river divides Canada into eastern and western regions?..... 521

How does the climate of eastern Canada compare with that of Europe? With that of southwestern Canada?............. 522

Mention four mineral products of Canada.................... 522

Where does the Ottawa river rise? Into what does it empty? Between what provinces does it form the boundary?..... 551

Locate Montreal. Describe the city. Why was it so named?..546, 830

Describe the Victoria bridge. State its length...... 522, 546, 778-780

Give a short sketch of Ottawa—its location, important buildings, chief commercial enterprise............................. 551

What is the meaning of the name Toronto? Of what province is Toronto the capital?.............................844, 575

For what is Quebec especially noted? Why is it often called the Gibraltar of America?................................. 562

Of what Canadian province is Halifax the capital? For what is its harbor noted? What government station is maintained at Halifax?... 536

Name the terminals of the Canadian Pacific railroad........ 522

In what country is the Klondike gold region? What city is the business center of the Klondike?......................... 522

In what part of Canada was gold discovered in 1910?........... 748

Name the greatest grain and timber market in America. The
greatest lumber market in the world...................524, 521

Of what three natural divisions does Mexico consist? State its
extreme length and breadth. Mention its two highest
mountains... 543

Give the area and population of Mexico. How many states does
it contain? How many territories? Name the six most
populous states....................................... 543

Explain the signification of the following names: Costa Rica,
Guatemala, Honduras...............................810-820

Give a brief description of the isthmus of Panama. How high
is Culebra pass?...................................... 553

Describe the republic of Panama. Give its dimensions. Its
capital. Upon what foundation is the city built?........553, 552

Describe the climate of Panama. Mention its staple crop. What
is the character of the interior forests?.................... 553

What are the mineral resources of Panama? What is its chief export? 553

What is the Canal Zone? By whom is it controlled?........... 553

Give size and cost of the Panama canal. How much does it shorten
the sea route from New York to San Francisco?........... 553

Locate Porto Rico. Mention the capital. The metropolis.
Describe the people. What are the exports?............559-560

State the area of Cuba. Name its capital. Its chief export.
A metal found in large quantities...................527-528, 605

What portion of Cuba is mountainous? Tell something of the
climate of Cuba. The vegetation. The animal life.......527-528

What is the meaning of the name Havana? Describe the city
and the harbor. Name the principal manufacture......... 536

Where is Mt. Pelée? Describe the volcanic eruption of 1902..... 556

What are national parks? National monuments? Name and
locate ten of each.................................... 555

SOUTH AMERICA

Compare the area of South America with that of North America. 852

Give a brief description of the Andes mountains. For what
are they celebrated?................................... 509

Name three South American volcanoes. The highest mountain
on the American continent............................577, 547

Give a concise account of the Amazon river. How long is it?
How wide at its mouth? What is the area drained by it?.. 509

In what country and in what mountains does the Orinoco rise?
What length of coast line is intersected by its mouths?..... 551

Where is the La Plata river? Give some interesting facts about
its waters. Name two cities on its banks................. 564

What portion of South America is occupied by Brazil? Compare
the area of Brazil with that of Europe............520, 604, 852

Mention two facts concerning the rivers and forests of Brazil. .
What are the valuable woods? The chief minerals?........ 520

Describe Rio de Janeiro..................................... 564

State the length, breadth, and area of Argentina. Mention the
four chief natural divisions of its surface. Name its highest
mountain. Give its principal exports..................... 515

Where is Buenos Ayres? How does the city secure telegraphic
communication with North America?...................520-521

Locate Chile. State its width. What is the climate? Give its
chief source of wealth. What metal is abundant?......... 525

Name the capital of Chile. Two other cities................. 525

In what country is Mt. Cotopaxi? For what is it noted?....... 527

From what South American country do most of the diamonds
of commerce come? Much of the platinum?............520, 526

Compare the wool product of South America with that of the
United States. Of Canada. Name two grains produced in
large quantities in South America....................... 680

What is the origin or the meaning of the following: Argentina,
Brazil, Cape Horn, Chile, Patagonia, Peru?.............800-834

EUROPE

For what three features is the continent of Europe noteworthy?.. 531

Describe the climate of Europe. Name its chief mountain
systems. What are its principal rivers?.................. 531

What grand division is separated from Europe by the Caspian sea?
By the Mediterranean? By the Caucasus mountains?....523, 543

What boundary is partly formed by the Ural mountains? What
minerals and precious stone s are found in the Urals?....... 576

Why is the Caspian sea noted? Why is navigation perilous?..... 523

Locate the Dardanelles. How wide is it?..................... 528

Where are the Alps? Between what seas do they form a water-
shed?... 508

Name four passes of the Alps. Tell something of the Simplon
pass. Name three lesser peaks of the Alps...............508-509

Describe Mont Blanc. The Matterhorn...................545, 542

Define glacier. What are moraines? Name the largest glacier
in the world. The largest in Europe...................... 533

Give a brief description of the river Rhine.................... 563

In what forest does the Danube rise? Describe this river....... 528

What countries are separated by the English channel?.......... 530

State the name applied to the United Kingdom, with its colonies
and dependencies. What countries compose the United
Kingdom? Name its capital.....................534-535, 605

What are the boundaries of England? State its area. Tell
something of the river Thames.......................530, 574

Describe the climate of England. Mention six cities........... 530

Briefly describe London. What is its rank?.................. 540

Describe St. Paul's cathedral. Give a brief account of Westminster abbey. What is the "poets' corner"? For what is
Westminster hall chiefly remarkable?..........571, 579-580, 835

For what is each of these streets of London noted: Cheapside,
Maiden Lane, Mincing Lane, Paternoster Row, Piccadilly,
Regent street, Rotten Row, Scotland Yard, Whitechapel?..807-846

Where and what is Great Tom? Grosvenor square? Hyde park?
Mayfair? Pall Mall? Trafalgar square?..............817-844.

State three facts about the commerce of Liverpool and its shipping facilities.. 540

Give a brief description of Wales. Tell something of the people.
Of the valuable minerals. Mention three manufactures..... 577

Why are few points in Scotland more than forty miles from
the sea? How many islands does Scotland possess?....568-569

Name four chief cities of Scotland. Which is the capital?....569, 529

Describe the situation of Edinburgh. Why is it called the modern
Athens? Mention three points of interest in the city..529-530

For what is Glasgow celebrated?............................ 533

Describe the surface of Ireland. The climate. Why is Ireland
called the emerald isle? Why has the country few manufactures?... 538

Where and what is the Giant's causeway?................... 533

On what land is Dublin built? Describe the city............. 529

What are the boundaries of France? What great commercial
advantages does France possess because of its position?... 531

Compare the climate of France with that of other countries of
Europe. What product is a principal source of wealth?.... 531

Name the chief minerals of France. The principal manufactures.
For what is Sèvres noted? St. Gobain? Amiens?........531-532

Name the great commercial cities of France. The finest ports.. 532

Describe Paris—its situation, quays, fortifications, streets,
boulevards, triumphal arches, principal public square..554, 800

What is the Champs Elysées? The Bois de Boulogne? The
Bois de Vincennes?.............................806, 803, 554

Briefly describe the cathedral of Notre Dame. What is the
Panthéon at Paris? The Louvre?.................554-555, 826

How high is the Eiffel tower? By whom was it designed?.....530, 430

Give some facts about Cherbourg, Marseilles, Rheims. For what production is the vicinity of Rheims noted?........524-563

Why are the passes of the Pyrenees dangerous?.............. 562

Give the boundaries of Spain. Describe the interior............ 570

To what country does Gibraltar belong? Where is it? Compare it with other fortresses. Describe the strait of Gibraltar.533, 816

Name some of the principal minerals found in Spain. What portion of Spain is covered by forests? Name some remarkable trees. Mention five fruits grown in Spain........... 570

Compare Madrid with other European cities. Describe the city—its gates, principal street, greatest building, royal museum.. 541

Name the most important manufacturing city in Spain....... 518

For what is the harbor of Lisbon distinguished? Why has Lisbon no very old buildings?...........................540

Name the capital of France. Of Spain. Of Portugal........604-605

Give the origin of the following names: Bordeaux, Havre, Lisbon, Madrid, Portugal, Spain.......................803-842

Of how many provinces is Belgium composed? Mention an important fact concerning the farmers of Belgium....... 518

To whom is much of the coal of Belgium sold? Name three manufactures of Belgium. Where is each made?.......... 518

How is Brussels often described? Name some noted buildings... 520

For what is the cathedral at Antwerp celebrated?............ 510

Locate the Netherlands, or Holland. Mention six possessions of Holland... 548

Describe the surface of Holland. How far below sea-level are the lowest parts? For what two purposes are dikes used?... 548

On what foundation is Amsterdam built? Describe its mode of defense. For what expert workmen is Amsterdam famous? 509

Describe Rotterdam. For what is the Hague celebrated?....567, 536

Name the capital of Belgium. Of the Netherlands. Compare the areas of the two countries..........................604-605

What is the chief commercial city of the Netherlands? The chief port? Mention the chief port of Belgium......509, 567, 510

What is the Allée Verte? The Binnenhof?.................798, 803

Name four countries bordering on the Baltic sea............. 517

Of how many states is the German empire composed? Name five. 532

Describe the surface of Germany. Where is the Black forest?... 532

Name two mountain ranges of Germany. Five rivers. Tell how far south the Rhine freezes............................ 532

In what agricultural products does Germany excel? Name five principal seaports. Five commercial cities.........532, 680

Of what empire is Prussia the principal state? Name three important cities...................................... 561

Why is Berlin an important city? How does it rank with other cities of Europe? What is "Unter den Linden"?.......518, 845

Tell something about the cathedral at Cologne................. 526

Give three reasons for the importance of Hamburg............. 536

Describe Munich. Name its principal industries............547-548

What is the most famous institution in Dresden?.............. 529

By whom was each of the following cities founded: Cologne, Hamburg, Munich?...............................526-548, 830

Where is Oberammergau? For what is it celebrated?.......... 550

For what is Aix-la-Chapelle noted?........................... 798

Describe Denmark. Name four island possessions. Four seaports. How is internal communication carried on?..............528-529

Trace the history of the name Copenhagen..................809-810

Give the boundaries of Austria-Hungary. Its capital........517, 605

Tell something of the races and languages in Austria-Hungary... 517

Locate and briefly describe Vienna. For what is it noted?....... 577

Of what country is Budapest the capital? Contrast Buda and Pest as to position and character......................... 520

Compare Prague with Budapest. How did the name Prague originate?......................................560, 520, 836

Where is Carlsbad? For what is it noted? Ischl?...........523, 822

In the basin of what river does Rumania lie? Describe the climate. What is the chief occupation of the people?...... 567

Describe the surface of Switzerland. Are its rivers navigable? Name five lakes......................................573-574

Why is Lake Lucerne so named? What is the lion of Lucerne? Where is St. Bernard pass? Chillon?..................808-838

Describe the shape of Italy and its climate. Name its boundaries. Which province is called the garden of Italy?............ 538

What range of mountains intersects Italy? Describe Mt. Vesuvius. What cities have been destroyed by its eruptions?..538, 576

Give a brief description of the river Po. Of the Tiber.......558, 574

Where is Lake Maggiore? What island in it is renowned for its beauty?... 541

Describe Rome, mentioning the city gates, the finest streets, the palaces and villas, the vatican.....................565-567, 576

Compare St. Peter's cathedral with other churches...........571-572

By what name is the Pantheon now known? Describe it briefly. To what fact is the preservation of the Pantheon due?..566, 554

What cities does the Appian way connect? Where are the most celebrated catacombs found?....................800, 781

What is the Corso? The Porta Maggiore? The Quirinal?
Capitoline hill?..805-837
For what is the city of Naples noted? What does its name mean?
Where and what is Miseno?......................548, 830, 544
Why are Capri and Pompeii interesting? Carrara?....523, 558, 806
Give a brief description of Milan...........................543-544
Describe the situation of Genoa. Why is its architecture celebrated? 532
In what respects does Florence excel most other cities of Europe?
Give an account of the Ponte Vecchio..................531, 835
Upon what foundation is Venice built? Tell something of the
palace of the doges. Locate the bridge of sighs...... 576
What is a campanile? Give the history of the campanile of St.
Mark. Of the basilica of St. Mark.................576, 521, 828
Locate Pisa. How old is the city? Describe the leaning tower.558, 521
What is the Riviera?... 565
By what strait is Sicily separated from Italy? When was this
region devastated by an earthquake?...................538, 788
Describe Mt. Etna, mentioning its height, its circumference,
the life upon its slopes, and its most disastrous eruptions.. 530
Describe the coast of Norway. What mountains separate Norway
from Sweden? Name the plants of the mountain districts.. 550
Describe the surface of Norway. Name the chief industries of
the Norwegian people. Mention three cities of Norway... 550
Into what three regions is Sweden divided? Describe the surface.
The climate. The domestic animals..................... 573
What portion of Sweden is cultivated? With what countries
does Sweden carry on most of its trade?................ 573
Describe Stockholm. Of what does its commerce consist?...... 571
Give the area of Russia. Describe the climate, the soil, and the
surface of European Russia.............................567-568
Locate the Valdai hills. Where does the Volga river rise?....568, 577
From what mountains does Russia secure most of her minerals?
In what part of Russia are there extensive petroleum wells? 568
How does Russia rank with other countries in extent, power,
and population? With what countries is most of the com-
merce carried on?.....................................567-568
Mention five of the largest cities of Russia. Which are the capitals
of Russia?..567-568
Describe Petrograd—the river, the quay, the bridges, the fortress.
At what times is the city inundated?..................... 572
Name five public buildings of Petrograd. Tell something of St.
Isaac's cathedral. Nevskii Prospekt? Tsarskoe Selo?
Cronstadt?................................572, 831-844, 527

How far from Petrograd is Moscow? What part of Moscow does
    the Kremlin occupy? Describe the great bell......547, 824, **777**
Where is Warsaw? How is it connected with Praga?........577-578
Of what is Turkey in Europe composed? Describe the surface.
    What is the climate?................................575-576
Name some attractions of Constantinople. Give its Turkish name.
    Of what are the houses built? Name two great buildings.
    What is the golden gate? The sublime porte?......526, 817, 842
Mention three divisions of Greece. Describe the shores and the
    surface. Mention six plants cultivated there............. 536
Mention the remains of ancient buildings in Athens...........515-516
Name the capitals of Greece, Turkey, Norway, and Sweden....604-605
What city is the greatest commercial port on the continent of
    Europe? What European country exports large quantities
    of vegetable seeds?................................536, 548
Name the longest river in Europe. The highest mountain.....564, 547

ASIA

Give the location and dimensions of Asia. What proportion of
    the land surface of the globe does it occupy?.............. 515
State the total population of Asia. What proportion of the
    earth's inhabitants does it include?..................... 515
Name ten great rivers of Asia. Which is longest? What four
    world rivers exceed all those of Asia? Name the chief Asian
    fresh-water lakes................................515, 564-565
Where are the Himalaya mountains? How high upon the
    Himalayas is vegetation found? The highest human habi-
    tation? Name three important peaks..................536-537
Give the area of Siberia. Of what commercial value are the
    river systems? What is the soil of southern Siberia?.....567-568
Omitting Arabia, of what does Turkey in Asia mainly consist?.. 576
Give a brief description of the Euphrates river. What is the
    origin of its name? Why is the Tigris so called?......531, 814, 844
Where is Palestine? To what empire does it now belong? Name
    the principal cities of Palestine. Describe Jerusalem......552, 539
Where is the Dead sea? Are its waters salt or fresh? Give the
    level of its surface. What noted river empties into it? ...528, 539
Where is Mount Carmel? What does its name mean? Locate
    the land of Canaan................................523, 805
For what is Mecca celebrated? Give facts about Medina......542-543
With what countries and in what way is most of the commerce
    of Persia carried on? Name a most important staple....... 556
Give the boundaries of India. Name five cities............. 537

What are the Hindu beliefs in regard to the Ganges?........... 532

For what is Calcutta chiefly noted? How does it compare with capitals of Europe?..................................... 521

Give a short description of Rangoon......................... 562

Give a brief description of the Taj Mahal. In what country is it? By whom was it built? Tell something of Shah Jehan....................................574, 843, 487

Where and what is Mandalay? The Punjab? Golconda? Give the origin of Bombay, Calcutta, and Ganges............. 803-836

Locate Ceylon. To what country does it belong? Name five native animals. Five food plants........................ 524

Of what kingdom is Bangkok the capital? Describe the walls of Bangkok. The native houses. How is the internal traffic of the city carried on?........................ 517-518

What is Singapore? Give the meaning of the name........... 841

How does the area of China compare with that of the whole of Asia? What are the four divisions of the Chinese republic? State its population................................... 525

Give the location of the Yellow sea, and tell why it is so named.. 580

Give the boundaries of China proper. Name the four principal rivers. Describe the Yang-tse-kiang.................. 525, 580

Where is the great wall of China? The grand canal?..... 817, 525

What is the climate of China? What are the principal agricultural products? The principal manufactures?.................. 525

How is trade carried on by China with Russia? With Europe and America?.. 525

Where and what is Port Arthur?............................ 559

Name five cities of China. Designate the capital.............. 525

Describe the construction of Peking. What is its population?. 555-556

By what two classes is Canton inhabited? How are they separated? Give some facts about the streets............. 522

What are the characteristic features of Shanghai? Why is it an important city?..................................... 569

Where and what is Hong-Kong? For what is it notable?...... 537

Name the four principal islands of Japan. What name have the Japanese given to their empire?..................... 539

Give the dimensions of Nippon. Describe the coasts, the surface, and the climate of Japan. Why is the plant life varied? Name some products of the north. The south............ 539

What agricultural product is the chief food article of Japan? Of what is Japanese paper made?...................... 539

Name five principal cities of Japan. Describe Tokyo. What is the Asakasa pagoda?........................539, 575, 800

Where is Osaka? Tell something of the castle of Osaka....... 551
Describe Yokohama. Name the principal exports and imports. 581
What can you say of the volcanic and earthquake destruction
    of the cities of Japan? What and where is Fuji-yama?...539, 816

AFRICA

At what point is the distance between Europe and Africa least?
    How is Africa united to Asia?........................... 507
Why is the Red sea remarkable? Give origin of its name....563, 837
By what sea is the northern coast of Africa washed?........... 507
Name in order of size the four great rivers of Africa......564-565, 581
Briefly describe the Nile. What is its total length?.......549-550, 831
Where is the Zambezi river? State the area of its basin. Where
    are the Victoria falls? What American waterfall is rivaled
    by the Victoria falls?................................847, 581
Locate Lake Victoria Nyanza. Albert Nyanza.............576-577
Describe the vegetation of Africa. Name two animals peculiar
    to Africa. Give an account of the races found in Africa... 507
Name two independent governments existing in Africa. By
    what European countries is most of Africa dominated?..507-508
What are some of the exports of Africa?...................... 508
Where is Morocco? How does the climate east of the Atlas
    mountains differ from that on the west?.................. 546
Of what country is Algiers the capital? Why is it called the
    silver city? At what season is it a resort for English people? 508
Name three physical divisions of Egypt. Which is chiefly
    cultivated? Give a reason for the fertility of the delta.... 530
Describe the climate of Egypt. Mention three native trees.
    Three mineral deposits.................................. 530
Where is Cairo? State the nationalities of its residents........ 521
Where are the pyramids? Describe them. By whom and for
    what purpose were they built? Where is Ghizeh?.......561, 521
Describe the Suez canal. What waters does it connect? Name
    its terminal cities...................................... 573
How much is the voyage from Europe to India shortened by the
    Suez canal? Is the canal closed in time of war?........... 573
Of what two provinces is southern Rhodesia composed? What
    territory is included in northern Rhodesia? For whom is
    Rhodesia named? What is the area of the gold fields?....563-564
What provinces form the Union of South Africa? In general,
    what is the surface of the region? Its climate?............ 570
Locate the province of Cape of Good Hope. What is its most
    valuable mineral? Name the chief exports................ 522

Where are the gold coast, Pompey's pillar, the pillars of Hercules?
For whom were Pietermaritzburg and Pretoria named?.817-836

GENERAL QUESTIONS

When it is 12 o'clock noon according to eastern time in the
United States, what time is it according to central time?
Mountain time? Pacific time?......................... 850
When it is 12 o'clock noon according to eastern time in the
United States, what time is it at London? At Berlin?
At St. Petersburg?................................... 850
Name the five longest rivers in the world, and arrange them in
the order of their size................................564-565
What is the travel distance by steamer from San Francisco to
Manila? New York to Suez? Montreal to Liverpool?...864-865
Name in order of size the ten largest cities in the world........ 582
What places were destroyed by the three most disastrous earth-
quakes of the 18th century? Name five of the most destruc-
tive earthquakes of the 19th century. One of the 20th...786-788
Where is silver most abundant? Compare the silver mines of
America with those of Europe and Asia................... 765
How many miles would one travel by steamship in going from
Liverpool to Cape Town? Boston to Bermuda? New York
to Havre?...864-865
What country produces more wool than any other country in
the world? Potatoes? Beet sugar? Corn? Rice?....... 680
Compare the production of rye in the United States with that
of Russia.. 680
How does the production of wheat in the United States compare
with that of Russia? British India? France? Canada?... 680
Name the five largest lakes in the world. Which of the great lakes of
the world is the highest above sea-level? Which is the deepest? 539
State the travel distance by steamship from San Francisco to
Honolulu. New York to Liverpool. London to Mel-
bourne. New York to Rio de Janeiro.................864-865
Which is the longest ship canal in the world? In Europe?..... 654
Name the largest island in the world. The highest mountain.
The longest river..........................   ....516, 547, 564
What is the travel distance from Quebec to Vancouver? Toronto
to Muskoka? Boston to Halifax? Montreal to Winnipeg?.. 866
Name the highest volcano in the world. Mention three volcanoes
of South America. Three of North America. Where is Mauna
Loa? Teneriffe? Stromboli? Elburz? Kilima-Njaro?
Kilauea?... 577

GOVERNMENT—General

What country governs the largest number of people? Which controls the greatest area?............................604-605

Give the titles of the rulers of the United Kingdom, France, Egypt, Persia, Turkey, China.................................. 605

In whom is the executive power of the British empire vested? What body exercises complete legislative power?....... 590

Name the two houses of the British parliament. How long does a parliament last? How often do its members meet?........ 590

How do the members of the British house of lords acquire their office? How many members are there?.................. 590

How many members constitute the British house of commons? How are they chosen?................................ 590

State some changes made in the British constitution in 1911... 590

Of what officers does the cabinet of Great Britain consist?....... 590

Outline the local government of Scotland..................... 622

Give the title and the duties of the chief executive of Ireland.... 606

Name three classes of colonies belonging to the British empire. Explain how their forms of government differ......... 590

Mention a British crown colony in Asia. In Africa. In Europe.. 534

Name two British possessions which have representative government. Two having responsible government............ 534

How is Gibraltar governed? The Bermudas? New Zealand? Zanzibar?......................................534, 590, 614, 642

Name the chief executive of Canada.......................534, 591

Name the houses of the Canadian parliament. What are the salaries of the members?................................ 591

Give three qualifications required of the Canadian senator. What is his term of office?.................................... 591

By whom is the governor-general of Canada appointed? State his term of office and salary. The premier's salary.......591-592

Name the heads of departments by whom the governor-general of Canada is assisted..................................591-592

Outline the local government throughout the Dominion of Canada. On what models are the courts based?..................... 592

Which British cabinet officer has charge of the administration of the affairs of India? How long does the viceroy hold office? What salary does he receive?.................... 606

Give in full the official title of the ruler of the British empire... 590

What important positions under the British government have been held by the following: Sir Robert Peel, Disraeli, Gladstone, Marquis of Salisbury, Earl of Rosebery, A. J. Balfour, Sir Henry Campbell-Bannerman, H. H. Asquith?.........400-485

For what service in the government of Great Britain is John Morley noted? Joseph Chamberlain? James Bryce? David Lloyd-George? Cecil Arthur Spring-Rice?..............412-490

With what country is the name of Edmund Burke associated? Daniel O'Connell? John Dillon?......................413-472

Upon what decree is the constitution of the German empire based? What are the prerogatives of the German emperor? By whom may government officials be dismissed?......... 602

Name the two legislative bodies of Germany. Of how many members does each consist?............................. 602

How was Wilhelm I chosen emperor of Germany? Give date. 602

Name the imperial secretaries through whom the government of the German empire is administered................602-603

Describe the government of Austria-Hungary. In what matters are the governments of Austria and Hungary separately conducted? In what matters united?..................... 589

Where do the lawmaking bodies of Austria-Hungary meet?...... 589

What kind of monarchy existed in Russia previous to 1917? What form of government was first substituted for it?.... 621

When was the Russian duma created? State the term of office and the salary of the members............................ 621

Compare the Russian council of the empire with the duma. Could either body pass a measure rejected by the emperor?........ 621

What was the ruling senate of Russia? The holy synod?....... 622

What was an avowed object of the revolution of 1917?......... 622

Name the divisions of the legislature of France. Who elects the president of France? What is his salary?................ 602

State the number of members in the senate of Italy. How long do they serve? What power has the king over the chamber of deputies? What compensation do legislators receive?.... 607

Describe the body known in Spain as the cortes. In what year did Spain make military service compulsory?.............. 623

What form of government does Portugal now have? How often may the constitution be revised?..................... 617

Why is Belgium called a neutral power? How is failure to vote treated? How many votes may one person cast?.......... 589

State the property qualification for membership in the upper house of the states general of the Netherlands........... 612

What form of government was proclaimed for Bulgaria in 1908? 590

What is the Norwegian storthing? How may the king's veto
be overridden?.. 615

In what matters has the king of Sweden legislative power?
Who may impose taxes?................................ 632

Give an outline of the manner in which Denmark is governed. 601

By the constitution of 1864 who controlled the legislative power
of Greece? What change was made in 1911?........... 603

Of how many cantons is Switzerland composed? What powers
have the Swiss people under the "initiative"? What official
serves as chief executive of Switzerland?.................. 632

By what code are the powers of the sultan of Turkey restricted?
What authority has the grand vizier?..................... 632

What income must a senator have in Rumania? Describe the
three classes of voters................................620-621

What form of government has Montenegro? Servia?.........611, 622

Where is Monaco? How is it governed?..................... 611

Name the form of government in China. When was it established?
What officers are included in the cabinet?................. 593

What is the standard of currency in China? The German
empire? Japan?.. 604

By what instrument are the powers of the ruler of Japan modified?
How many legislative houses has Japan? Of whom is
the house of peers composed?............................ 607

What is the relation of Korea to Japan?...................... 599

In what year was the first national council established in Persia?
What powers has it?.................................... 617

How is Afghanistan divided politically? Describe the government of the provinces. Give the title of the ruler...... 585

Name some provisions of the treaty confirmed in 1905 between
Afghanistan and Great Britain........................... 585

Give the population of Siam. How is it governed? When
does the legislative council meet?.....................604, 623

Name two European countries controlling more than half of
Africa. By what country is Egypt governed? The Union
of South Africa? Tripoli?................................508

How does the power of the ruler of Morocco differ from that of
the sultan of Turkey? Name the ministers. When are
they consulted?..611-612

What form of government has Liberia? By whom is it peopled?
After what is its constitution modeled?.................. 608

Into how many states is Mexico divided? Of whom is the congress
composed? Who may vote for legislators? How is a vacancy
in the office of president to be filled?..................... 609

When was the republic of Panama constituted? For how long a term is the president elected?............................ 616

Upon what conditions was the government of Cuba transferred from the United States to the Cuban people?.............. 599

How many coaling stations does the United States maintain in Cuba? At what annual cost?........................ 599

How is Hayti governed?..................................... 603

Where is Santo Domingo? What relation has its government to that of the United States?........................... 601

What form of government has Colombia? What provision is made for vacancy in the office of ruler?.................. 593

Who may vote in Bolivia? In Chile? In Ecuador?..........589-601

How and on what date is the president of Chile elected?........ 592

What is the government of Brazil? How are the senators elected?..589-590

For how long is the president of Argentina elected?............ 585

What are the qualifications for the office of president of Venezuela? Can he succeed himself?......................... 641

How long has Peru been a republic? Give details of its government. How many vice-presidents has it? State their salary. 617

How many central American states are there? Name them. How are they governed?..............................604-605

Of whom does the permanent court of arbitration at the Hague consist? What cases are referred to the Hague tribunal?.... 603

State the size of the United States army on April 1, 1917. To about what number did it increase during the first year of the war against Germany? What three main divisions were consolidated to form the United States army?................ 775

Of how many officers and men does a regiment consist? A rifle company? An infantry division?. 775

State the number of national army cantonments established during the first year of the war with Germany. The number of national guard camps.................................... 776

How many men joined the United States navy during the first year of war with Germany? What remarkable naval appropriations were made? Compare with earlier appropriations. 776

Name the departments of the United States navy. Locate the navy yards and naval stations........................... 776

What officer in the navy corresponds in rank to a general in the army? To a colonel? To a captain?.................... 776

For how long a term is the president of France elected? Of Argentina? Of Chile? Of Switzerland?................585-632

Give the form of government of Bolivia, Japan, Persia........589-617

CIVICS

On what is the government of the United States based?.... 632

Name six objects of the constitution of the United States... 594

How many amendments to the constitution have been made? What persons are citizens according to the 14th amendment? What is the 15th amendment?........................597-599

By what name is the 16th amendment to the constitution known? 599

Name three departments of the government of the United States. 633

Of what does the legislative department consist?.............. 633

How many senators are elected from each state? Of how many members is the United States senate composed?.........633, 624

By whom are United States senators elected? Which amendment to the constitution provides for their election?........633, 599

State the term of office of a United States senator. His salary. Who is eligible to this office? Who acts as president of the senate? 633

Who presides over the senate when it sits as a court of impeachment for the trial of the president of the United States?... 635

What provision is made in the 14th amendment for the apportionment of representatives? How many members constitute the present house of representatives?...................598, 633

By whom and for how long a term is a member of the house of representatives elected? Name three qualifications....... 633

State the powers of the house of representatives. Compare with the powers of the senate........................634, 633

What is the salary of a member of the house of representatives? Of the speaker?..................................... 634

What is the congress of the United States? What is the term of each congress? Name its general legislative powers...... 634

On what date does the regular annual session of congress begin? Who has the power of calling special sessions?............. 634

Who is the chief executive of the United States?............. 633

How old must the candidate for president be? How long a resident of the United States? Mention a third qualification. 634

When are state presidential electors chosen? To how many electors is each state entitled?......................634, 633

When and where do the state electors meet to vote for president? To whom must they submit certificates for their vote?.. 634

When and by whom are the votes of the state electors counted? 634

In case there is no choice by the state electors, by whom and how is the president of the United States then elected?... 634

What is the term of office of the president? What is his salary? 634

Name the powers and duties of the president.................. 634

When do acts of congress become laws? How many days are allowed the president in which to sign or veto any act? Can an act become a law after being vetoed by the president?.. 635

How is the vice-president of the United States elected? In case there is no choice by the state electors, by whom and how is the vice-president chosen?............................ 634

In case of death or removal from office of both president and vice-president, who would become president?............634-635

Name the ten divisions of the executive department of the government. How are the cabinet officers chosen?.............. 635

In what bodies is the judicial power of the United States vested? 633

By whom are justices of the United States courts chosen? For how long a term?................................. 635

Of how many members is the United States supreme court composed? State their salaries............................. 635

When does the supreme court convene? In what cases does it have original jurisdiction? Appellate jurisdiction?........ 635

Name the chief-justice and the associate judges who constitute the supreme court. Who was the first chief-justice?..... 640

Name five kinds of inferior courts of the United States. In what cases do these inferior courts have jurisdiction?...635-636

When and for what purpose were the United States circuit courts of appeals organized? Of whom is each composed?........ 635

How many judicial districts of the United States district courts are there?.. 635

What is the jurisdiction of the court of claims? The court of customs appeals? The commerce court?................. 636

Outline the duties of the secretary of state. Of the secretary of the treasury.. 636

What matters are in charge of the secretary of war? Name an institution under his supervision......................... 637

Of what department is the attorney-general the head?.....637-638

In what year was the postmaster-general first considered a cabinet officer? State his duties............................639, 638

What matters are under the supervision of the department of the interior? When was this department created?...... 638

Explain the nature of the business under the supervision of the secretary of agriculture. Of commerce. Of labor.......639-640

Name the present cabinet officers...........................636-640

When was the parcel post system provided for by congress? Who was postmaster-general at that time?..............848, 639

What cabinet positions were held by the following: George
Bancroft, Jefferson Davis, U. S. Grant, Carl Schurz, Daniel
Webster? For what was each distinguished?....636-639, 403-499
Who is the present speaker of the house of representatives?
How long was Joseph G. Cannon speaker?.............640, 415
Who is commander-in-chief of the army and the navy?...... 634
Name three men each of whom has on three occasions been a
candidate for the presidency of the United States. State
the political parties represented by them...............618-620
Which president received the largest popular vote? The largest
electoral vote?..618-620
Compare the popular vote of the following candidates for presi-
dent in 1912: Woodrow Wilson, Wm. H. Taft, Theodore
Roosevelt. For Woodrow Wilson and Chas. E. Hughes in 1916. 620
Name in order the three states having the largest number of
electoral votes. How many has your state? What is its
voting population?....................................626-631
What is the voting population of the state of New York?......628-629
Compare the voting population of California with that of Missouri.
Of Florida with that of Georgia........................626-629
What previous residence is required in your state, county,
town, and precinct in order to be eligible to vote?........626-631
What are the requirements as to citizenship of voters in your
state? What persons are not allowed to vote in your state?.626-631
In which states have women full suffrage?...........633, 626-627
Mention two states in which the voter must be able to read.626-631
Give the salary of your governor. His term of office.........626-631
The governor of which state receives the largest salary? Which
has the shortest term of office?........................626-631
How many years immediately preceding the election must a
candidate for governor of Massachusetts have resided in
the state? Of New York?........................609, 613-614
Mention three states in which the governor is not eligible for
election for the next succeeding term...............610, 613, 616
How often does the legislature of your state meet in regular
session? What is the term of office of the members?.....626-631
Is there a limit to the length of the regular session of the legisla-
ture in your state? If so, what?......................626-631
For how long a term are state senators elected in your state?
Members of the lower house of the legislature? What sala-
ries do they receive?.................................626-631
By what name is the legislature of Colorado known? Louisiana?
Massachusetts?...............................593, 608, 609

137

What is the age qualification for a member of the New York legislature? Of South Dakota?..........................614, 623

In what year did Oregon adopt the initiative and referendum?
Explain what these terms mean........................ 616

In what year was the initiative and referendum adopted by
Arkansas? By California?...........................585, 591

State some changes made in the constitutions of the following
states in 1912: Nebraska, Nevada, Ohio, Washington.....612-642

What public officials are subject to recall in Arizona? California? Colorado?.................................585-593

What officials are not subject to recall in Washington? Idaho?..642, 603

In what respects is the constitution of Oklahoma notable?... 615

How may the constitution of California be amended? Of Pennsylvania? Of Tennessee?.........................591, 616, 632

By whom are the laws for the District of Columbia made? How
do the officials obtain their offices?...................... 601

State one fact concerning suffrage in the District of Columbia. 630

For how long a term and by whom are territorial governors
appointed? How many delegates to congress has each
territory? Do the delegates have the right to vote?..... 633

What city is the seat of government in Alaska?................ 508

Does Hawaii have a legislature?............................. 633

Explain how a territory becomes a state...................... 633

Do untaxed Indians have the right to vote?.............633, 626-631

Who has authority to declare war? To grant pardons for offenses
against the United States? To establish post offices?...... 634

Name three cabinet members who cannot succeed to the presidency in case of vacancy. Give the reason.............634-635

Where must a crime against the United States be tried?........ 635

By whom was the date of inauguration day fixed?.............. 794

What is the unit of local government in New England? In
the South? In the western states?...................... 633

For what is each of the following names well known: John
Barrett, David J. Brewer, William Jennings Bryan, Joseph
H. Choate, John Watson Foster, John Hay, Philander C.
Knox, Whitelaw Reid, Elihu Root, Andrew D. White?..403-501

State one distinguishing fact about each of these: Augustus
Octavius Bacon, Champ Clark, Henry Cabot Lodge, Sereno
E. Payne, Thomas B. Reed, Oscar W. Underwood....402-496

Tell something of each of the following: Albert J. Beveridge,
Joseph W. Folk, J. Frank Hanly, Charles E. Hughes, Hiram
W. Johnson, Martin Augustine Knapp, Thomas R. Marshall,
Benjamin R. Tillman.................................406-494

INDUSTRY—INVENTION—COMMERCE

Name in order of the gross value of their products the three
   greatest industries of the United States..............661-662
Which industry of the United States has the most establishments?
   The greatest number of employees?.....................661-662
Is iron found in a pure state? Name three iron ores.......672, 673
What is cast iron? Pig iron? Which of the United States pro-
   duces the most pig iron? Which country of the world?.....   673
Explain two processes of making steel from cast iron. When and
   by whom was each process invented?..............673, 668, 670
State the effect of the introduction of the Bessemer process upon
   the iron and steel trade. When was this process introduced
   into the United States by Andrew Carnegie?............406, 416
Name the country producing the most steel. What is the value
   of the iron and steel exported by the United States?......673, 662
Name the inventor of the open-hearth steel process. Of nickel
   steel..671, 672
How does malleable iron differ from steel? What are the proper-
   ties of malleable iron?................................672-673
Give the meaning of the term cutlery. From what metal are
   razors made? How are they tempered? How hardened?..   660
Give the forest area of the United States. State the amount of
   timber taken annually from the forests, and its value. Give
   the annual value of the wood product..................660-661
Compare the number of persons in the United States employed in
   making bread and other bakery products with those manu-
   facturing tobacco.....................................661-662
How does the making of flour and other grist mill products rank
   among the industries of the United States?...............   661
Name the most valuable export of the United States. The most
   valuable import......................................662-663
Describe the cotton plant. In what latitudes does it thrive?
   Mention three species, and tell in what countries each grows.658-659
Distinguish two varieties of cotton cultivated in the United States.
   Which forms the bulk of American cotton?...............   659
When was sea island cotton introduced into the United States?
   From what place? In what two states is it cultivated?..   659
During what months is the cotton crop of the United States
   harvested? Name two uses of cotton seeds...............   659
Give the steps in the manufacture of cotton yarn..............   659

By whom and when was the spinning-jenny invented? The water frame? The mule spinner? The power loom? The cotton gin? The round bale cotton press?..........659, 668-672

Give some facts about Richard Arkwright, Edmund Cartwright, Samuel Crompton, J. M. Jacquard, Eli Whitney..........399-501

How does the United States rank as a wool producing country? Which is greater—its export of wool or its import?..680, 662-663

Of what does coal mainly consist? How was it formed? Mention three varieties of coal in common use. What is lignite?... 655

Give the area of the coal fields of the United States. Of China and Japan... 655

How many of the United States produce anthracite coal? Bituminous coal?...655-656

State the approximate value of the annual coal export of the United States...................................... 662

How is coke obtained? Coal tar? Mention seven coal-tar products..658, 656

When was the miner's safety lamp invented? Tell something of the inventor..669, 425

Mention five leading agricultural products of the United States. Name the state excelling in each......................648-649

What kind of plow was invented in 1784? When and by whom were the following invented: grain threshing-machine, "McCormick" reaper, sulky plow, grain-binder, self-binding reaper, rotary disk cultivator, automatic grain-binder, steam plow, electric plow, automobile mower?...........668-672

Of which orchard fruits has the United States the largest yield? What is the value of the grape crop?..................... 650

Name four countries of Europe in which making sugar from the beet is an important industry.....................734-735

What is meant by adulteration? State the chief objects of adulteration. In what manner are butter, cheese, milk, lard, cocoa, coffee, spices, honey, and vinegar adulterated?...... 645

In what century and where was paper invented? When was the first paper mill built in America?....................62, 668

In what year was Hoe's lightning press invented? State its speed. Who invented the linotype machine?............670, 672

Mention the principal achievements of Johann Gutenberg, Robert Hoe, Ottmar Mergenthaler......................441-465

How does the printing and publishing business of the United States rank as an industry?............................ 661

Of what is printer's type made? What is a font? In English, which letter occurs most frequently?...................678-679

By whom was the first steamboat in the United States built? The first steam road wagon? When was the first successful steamboat built in Europe?............................668, 88

Name the builder of the first steamboat to navigate the Hudson. Of the first to make a trip to sea. Name the first sea-going ironclad war vessel. The first steamship to cross the Atlantic..668-670, 88

When was the first oil-burning steamship built? The first electric locomotive?.....................................   672

What keeps a locomotive on the track? What kind of iron is used for rails?..   674

Name the inventor of the automatic air brake. The automatic car coupler. The sleeping car........................671, 670

Tell something of the following men and their inventions: Denis Papin, James Watt, Robert Fulton, George Stephenson, John Ericsson, George Westinghouse....................431-500

When and by whom was the cable car invented? When was the first standard electric railway in the United States built?..670, 672

Name the inventor of the lightning conductor. The electric battery. The storage battery......................668, 671

Who invented the telegraph? Give date of first message sent. Where was the first commercial telegraph built?.....670, 675-676

Give a brief description of the apparatus for telegraphic communication. What system of telegraphy is most extensively used?..   675

Name the inventor of the wireless telegraph. Mention three methods of wireless telegraphy...........................   676

By whom and when was the telephone invented? Explain its working. Is the voice carried over the wire?........671, 676-677

In what year was the wireless telephone invented? The tungsten electric light?.....................................   672

Give a brief account of the lives and inventions of Marconi, Morse, Tesla, Volta....................................462-497

Explain the telescope and its use. By whom were the first telescopes made? Name two of the largest refractors in the world...677-678

When was the daguerreotype invented? Color photography?..669, 672

Name four kinds of clay used for various industrial purposes. For what is fire clay used? Who was Bernard Palissy?..655, 473

What improvement did Fahrenheit make in the thermometer? Name an invention made by Torricelli. When and in what country did each live?..........................432, 668, 495

What invention by Daimler led to the development of the motor car or automobile?.....................................   651

Give figures showing the remarkable growth of the automobile industry in the United States. How many motor vehicles were manufactured in 1917? For how many did the industry provide a livelihood?................................651-652

Mention noted aeroplane flights made in Europe and America. What is the hydro-aeroplane?.........................646, 672

Give some facts about the inventions and achievements of the Wright brothers, Santos-Dumont, Glenn H. Curtiss...424-504, 672

When and by whom was the phonograph invented? The kinetoscope? The kinetophone?............................671-672

Give brief sketches of the lives of Alexander Graham Bell and Thomas A. Edison..................................405, 429

Name two countries in which canals were in use in remote times. Explain the workings of the lock system................652-653

By whom were friction matches invented? Safety matches? The revolver? Smokeless gunpowder?..................669-671

For what line of invention and its development are Colt, Gatling, and Krupp noted?..................................421-454

With what European country is the commerce of the United States greatest?..663-664

Name three European countries whose imports exceed their exports. 663

Compare the total value of the exports of the United States with the total value of the imports.....................662-663

Name some metals that have been used for making coins....... 656

What metal is commonly used as an alloy? What proportion of alloy is used in the United States? In Great Britain?.. 656

State the value of the franc in United States money. Of the mark. Of the yen. Of the pound sterling................ 657

State the value in United States money of a peso of each of the following countries: Argentina, Chile, Mexico, Uruguay.... 657

When was the present system of national banks established? State the minimum capital required in towns of different sizes. 652

Tell something of the required deposit of bonds and the issue of circulating notes of national banks........................ 652

Give the provisions of the currency law of 1913................ 652

What is a clearing house?................................... 655

Define interest. Why is interest high when profits are high? What is the legal rate of interest in your state?........665-666

In how many years does a note become outlawed in your state? A judgment?... 667

Associate each of the following with some branch of industrial or commercial life: Henry Clews, Marshall Field, Henry C. Frick, James J. Hill, J. P. Morgan, Henry Phipps....420-476

142

SCIENCE—EDUCATION—FINE ARTS

Define science. Distinguish between theoretical and practical science.. 722

Name six abstract sciences. Of what does each treat? Mention four concrete sciences..............................722-723

To what does mathematics relate?......................... 722

What is meant by dynamics? Statics? The law of continuity? Cosmogony?...................................710, 707, 708

Name nine subjects included in physics...................... 723

What is the sun? Tell its diameter, its density, its mass, its inclination, its movement.............................. 725

State theories of the constitution of the sun, the nature of its envelopes and spots..,................................ 725

How far away are the stars? Classify them.................724-725

What are constellations? Name five........................ 707

Tell something of asteroids. Aerolites. Comets........687, 683, 706

Mention a discovery made or a theory advanced by Copernicus, Galileo, Kepler, Laplace, Gauss, Barnard................403-455

Define acoustics. Upon what does the transmission of sound depend?... 683

State the difference between a noise and a musical sound. Upon what does the pitch of a tone depend?.................... 683

Does sound travel faster through air or through water?........ 683

How fast does light travel? How is its intensity affected by the distance of the luminous object?...................714-715

Upon what does the color of an object depend? Name the primary colors. What are complementary colors?......... 705

Explain the process of color photography..................... 705

What is contractile force? Why is a tire heated before it is placed on a wheel?.................................... 707

Define horse power. How may the horse power of an engine be determined?..713-714

Explain the phenomena of capillary action.................689-690

What is meant by convection? Which heats more quickly—gas or liquid? Why can a fire be built on the ice?....... 708

What is meant by correlation of physical forces?.............. 708

Discuss the nature of electricity. Define conductor, non-conductor, insulation. Name the best conductors.........710, 706

State the difference between a motor and a dynamo. How may a dynamo be used as a motor?....................710-711

When and by whom was the electric current first converted into
mechanical motion?.................................669, 432

Trace the course of the electric current employed in running a
trolley car. When and by whom was the contact device
for the trolley invented?.............................711, 672

Tell the principle of the incandescent light. The arc light.....711-712

By whom and when was the first incandescent lamp invented?
The carbon filament for the electric lamp?..............669, 671

Why is the air removed from the bulb of the incandescent electric
light?... 711

How are X-rays obtained? Name the discoverer............726, 672

State the progress along scientific lines made by Galvani, Ampère,
Ohm, Joseph Henry, Joule, Faraday, Sir Wm. Thomson,
Sir Wm. Crookes, Roentgen, Elihu Thomson............397-494

What is distillation?...................................... 709

What three discoveries did the alchemists seek? Name a modern
science developed largely from alchemy................... 684

Define chemistry. What are compounds? Elements? What is
chemical affinity?....................................... 692

Name and explain three classes of chemical changes. Upon
what conditions do chemical changes depend?...........692-693

State the composition of water. What does atomic weight mean?
Give the atomic weight of oxygen. Of hydrogen........693, 694

Define atom. Explain the atomic theory. State its three laws. 687

Name an element found in all organic bodies. Name five carbon
compounds. What is the purest form of carbon? State its
atomic weight. Its specific gravity................693, 690, 694

Explain the process of combustion. What is spontaneous combustion? How does it usually take place?...............705-706

What is radium? By whom was it discovered?............... 674

Who discovered oxygen? When? What is ozone?..........694, 719

How is liquid air obtained? How is it used?.................. 715

What are acids? Why is the term indefinite?................. 683

Give the melting point of aluminium, iron, carbon............. 694

What is the common name of oxalic acid? Copper sulphate?
Calcium oxide? Sodium chloride?....................... 782

Of what is albumen composed? Name one abundant form...... 684

What is biology? Name its divisions........................ 723

Of what does the skeleton of mammalia consist?.............. 724

Name and describe the two layers of which the skin is composed.
State its functions...................................... 724

Describe the process of respiration in man. State its object.
Describe the structure of the lungs....................722, 715

Of what does blood consist? Describe two kinds of corpuscles in the blood of man.....................................688-689

Describe the chambers of the heart. Mention the valves. Name the movements of the heart...................... 713

What are arteries? Name the largest artery. Distinguish between arterial and venous blood. Trace the course of the blood through the circulation.....................686, 685, 696

Name the digestive organs. Describe the process of digestion. What is the alimentary canal?.....................709, 684-685

Of what does the nervous system consist? Name the principal parts of the brain. Give the number of cranial nerves. Of spinal nerves. At what speed is nervous energy transmitted? Is it identical with electricity?............................. 689

When was ether first used as an anæsthetic? Chloroform?...... 670

Who invented the ophthalmoscope? The pulmotor? What are they?......................................670, 444, 672

Mention some diseases caused by bacteria. By whom and when was the typhoid bacillus isolated? Tuberculosis? Diphtheria? Lockjaw?...............................730, 671-672

For what scientific progress is Berzelius noted? Lavoisier? Liebig? Pasteur? Dewar? Tripler? Harvey W. Wiley?.406-501

What has each of these contributed to medical progress or medical literature: Galen, Harvey, Jenner, Koch, Osler, Loeb, Carrel?.416-472

Of what does psychology treat? What theories have been advanced to account for dreams?.....................723, 710

Mention some of the writings of Lotze, Wm. James, Royce, Baldwin, Münsterberg, Meyer..........................402-483

What is mechanical engineering? Electrical? Marine?......... 712

Tell something of John Rennie, John A. Roebling, John Hays Hammond...442-481

What country has the greatest percentage of illiteracy?......... 714

Which country expends the most per capita for higher education? 788

Mention some ancient libraries. Which was most noted? Name the six greatest modern libraries.......................714, 684

Where and what is the Smithsonian institution? Cooper union? Carnegie institution?............................724, 708, 690

Where is Amherst college? Brown? Yale? Wellesley?......698-704

What educational work was accomplished by Pestalozzi? Froebel? 476, 435

For what is Charles William Eliot noted? Goldwin Smith? David Starr Jordan? Arthur T. Hadley? Abbott Lawrence Lowell?......................................430-488

Mention one work by Phidias. One by Praxiteles...........476, 478

Name some works of the following sculptors: Canova, Thorwaldsen, Crawford, Harriet Hosmer, Rodin, St. Gaudens, French, Borglum, Niehaus, Partridge...................410-494

What influence upon art was exerted by Cimabue? Giotto? Correggio?..420-437

For what was Michaelangelo celebrated? Da Vinci? Titian? Raphael? Guido Reni? Bernini?....................397-497

Name some masterpieces of Rubens, Van Dyck, Rembrandt, Murillo..469-496

Characterize the work of Velasquez, Ruysdaal, Gainesborough, Reynolds, Romney, Turner, Burne-Jones...............413-496

Tell something of West, Stuart, Trumbull...................491-500

Name some pictures by Sully, Boughton, Whistler, Blashfield, Abbey, Sargent.......................................393-500

For what is Rosa Bonheur famous? Corot? Meissonier? Bouguereau? Doré?................................409-465

Tell something of the work of Christy, Davenport, Fisher, Gibson, Pennell, Pyle, Remington.....................419-480

For what is the gallery at Dresden famous? At Brussels? The Berlin museum? The Antwerp cathedral?.............510-529

Who first reduced music to system? When was composition in harmony first introduced?............................718-719

Tell something of Handel, Bach, Haydn, Mozart, Cherubini, Beethoven, Rossini and Mendelssohn...................402-483

For what is Liszt celebrated? Dudley Buck? Paderewski? Richard Strauss?...................................412-491

Mention one composition by each: Wagner, Gounod, Brahms, Balfe...402-497

Tell something of the lives of Jenny Lind, Patti, Nordica, Melba, De Gogorza, Caruso, Tetrazzini.......................416-494

State the distinctive features of Egyptian architecture........ 511

When did Greek architecture flourish? Characterize it........511-512

Name two orders of Roman architecture. Three of Greek....512, 511

Name the features of Byzantine architecture. Of Saracenic... 512

Who originated the Gothic style? Name its essential element.. 512

Of what style is the cathedral at Cologne? The mosque of St. Sophia? Saint Chapelle, Paris?...................526, 569, 554

Describe St. Peter's cathedral. Name its style. Its architect.571-572

Describe the capitol at Washington. State the style of the treasury and pension buildings. The patent office. The congressional library................................578-579

Tell something of Sir Christopher Wren. Of Walter, Pelz, McKim, Carrère, and Lewis Nixon...............................416-503

NATURAL HISTORY

What are sponges?   Where do they come from?............... 766

Where are barnacles found?   What are they?................. 732

Name the parts of a lobster's body.   Compare the lobster and
the crab.   Where are the crab's teeth?.................750, 742

Describe the scorpion.   The spider.   How many legs has a
spider?   What is a tarantula?........................763, 766

Explain fully the structure of insects.   What is meant by meta-
morphosis?... 749

What are mining bees?   Carpenter bees?   Honey bees?   Where
do bumble bees lay their eggs?........................... 734

Describe the population of a beehive.   How is it governed?
How are the workers distinguished?   Which bees hum?
Which sting?.. 734

How is honey made?   Bee bread?   Wax?   Describe the development of the young bee.................................... 734

To what order do bees, ants, and wasps belong?............. 734

Of what and how do wasps make their nests?................. 769

Tell something of the habits of ants........................ 729

Describe the silkworm, its food, and its cocoon.   To what
country is it native?................................... 765

Give the life history of a butterfly.   What is a chrysalis?...738, 696

How are moths distinguished from butterflies?................ 753

How does a fly walk on the ceiling?   How long does it take a
fly to grow up?   What diseases are transferred by flies?. 746

Give the history and habits of the boll-weevil................. 737

Describe a land snail.   Name the edible snail.   Where do snails
lay their eggs?   What is conchology?..................765, 706

Describe the habitation and the growth of the oyster.......... 755

Describe the starfish.   Where is it found?..............766-767

Briefly describe a fish.   How does it breathe?   What is its chief
organ of progression?   Tell something of the fishes in
Mammoth cave....................................745, 541

Where is the bony pike found?   Describe it.................. 737

How large is a shark?   Mention three species.   Do sharks have
teeth?.. 764

How does a flying-fish fly?................................. 746

In what water does the salmon live?   State its size.   Its color.
Describe the different stages of its life.................. 763

To what size does the bass grow?   The bluefish?..........732, 736

Describe the flounder. The porgy. The shad...............746-764

Mention four animals classified as reptiles. In what respects are
reptiles and birds alike? Why are reptiles cold-blooded?.. 762

Distinguish between turtles and tortoises. Have the turtle's
eggs hard or soft shells? Where are they laid?......... 769

Where are the boa-constrictor and the python found? How do
they secure their food?............................737, 761

Briefly describe the crocodile. Is it found in America? Distinguish between the crocodile and the alligator......742-743, 729

What are amphibia? Name three. How do they breathe?..... 685

Name two animals classed as anura. Describe the development of a tadpole into a frog........................... 729

Where do frogs lay their eggs? Describe the tree-frog's feet.
What is a bullfrog?............................747, 729, 738

Distinguish between frogs and toads. Have they teeth? How
do toads protect themselves from their enemies?.......747, 768

State the general characteristics of birds. Name and describe
three orders of birds................................735-736

Why cannot the ostrich fly? What is the rhea?.............. 754

State the use of the pelican's pouch....................... 756

Where is the stork found? Describe its habits. Where does
the white stork build its nest?.......................... 767

Give the common name for the buzzard. The scientific name
of the hen hawk. What is its food?....................738-739

Describe the turkey vulture, or turkey buzzard. State its size. 768

To what family does the eagle belong? Mention four species.... 744

Where is the condor found? State its appearance, size, habits.. 742

Describe the partridge. The quail. Give their family name.755, 761

Name five birds of the pheasant family. Describe the peacock.
The habits of the true pheasant......................757, 756

From what country does the green parrot come? The parrakeet? 755

On what do owls feed? Woodpeckers?....................754, 771

Describe the nests of the crow, the meadow lark, the swallow,
the wren...743-771

Of what value to the farmer are the meadow lark and the crow?.752, 743

Describe the coloring of the bird of paradise, the blackbird, the
bluebird, the flamingo, the oriole......................735-754

Why is the bower-bird so named? To what country is it native?. 737

Give an account of the platypus and its mode of life......... 758

Describe the kangaroo. How does it travel? Where does it
live? How does the opossum carry its young?..........749, 754

From what part of the whale is whalebone obtained? Compare
the mouth of a whale with the mouth of a shark....769-770, 764

148

Is the porpoise a fish or a mammal? Describe it.............. 759
What is the manatee? Where is it found?.................... 751
Distinguish between the African and the Indian elephant. Which
    is domesticated?.. 744
Distinguish between the camel and the dromedary. To whom
    is the camel valuable?................................... 739
To what continent is the camelopard native? Describe it.. 739
Describe the deer. How is it distinguished from other rumi-
    nants? Where are deer chiefly found?................... 743
Of what value is the musk deer?............................ 753
Compare the chamois with the gazelle. With the goat.......741, 747
Describe the Rocky mountain sheep. What part of the world
    does the musk ox inhabit?........................764-765, 753
How large is the hippopotamus? To what domestic animal
    is it related?... 748
What is the most celebrated breed of horses? How is the age
    of a horse determined?...............................748-749
What are carnivora? Name three classes...................... 690
How many species of bear are found in North America?........ 733
For what are the raccoon and the sable prized?..............761, 762
Give the characteristics of the dog family. Mention three species
    of fox. Of wolf................................744, 746, 770
To what family do these belong: jaguar, leopard, lion, lynx,
    puma, tiger? Which are found in America?.............749-768
Distinguish between the seal and the walrus.................764, 769
Where is the beaver found? To what family does the beaver
    belong? The guinea pig? The squirrel?...........733, 748, 766
How does a flying squirrel fly?................................ 746
In what part of America is the porcupine found? Describe it. 759
On what food do bats live? Where is the vampire-bat found?. 733
Distinguish between apes and monkeys. Describe the Barbary
    ape, the orang-utan, the chimpanzee, the gorilla.......729-754
Define bacteria. Where are they found? Mention five forms... 730
Of what does moss consist? Describe its fruit...............752-753
Where do ferns grow most abundantly? To what height?
    Define cryptogamous, acrogen, frond, rhizome, circinate. 745
Describe the structure of a flower. What are double flowers?... 746
State the uses of barley. In what climates does it grow?.... 732
What plants grow best on calcareous clay?.................... 855
Describe sugar cane. How is it propagated?................. 767
Where do palms grow? Name the most valuable palms. Describe
    the cocoanut. State its uses. What is the betel nut? From
    what is sago obtained?......................755, 741, 735, 762

Name four species of pine. State where each grows. Name four pine products...................................757-758

What is Brazilwood? Redwood? Mahogany?.........737, 761, 751

Tell something of the orange tree. How productive is it? Where is it cultivated? To what country is the lemon native?..754, 750

From what fruits is the cultivated apple developed?.........729-730

What country is the home of the peach?...................... 756

How does tea grow? How is it prepared for market?........ 767

Describe the pepper plant. Where is it native? State the difference between black pepper and white pepper.....756-757

Relate briefly how coffee is grown. What country exports the best coffee? Name the greatest coffee producing country in the world..741-742

Where is the banana cultivated? How tall does it grow?...... 731

Describe the breadfruit. Where does it grow?................ 738

State the value of the bean as an article of food............ 733

Of how many layers is bark composed? What is cork? Peruvian bark?...731-732

What are cloves? From what are they obtained?............. 741

How tall does the pineapple plant grow? Name two localities in which it is extensively cultivated..................... 758

Explain how cocoa and cocoa butter are obtained.............. 739

What is manna?...751-752

What drug is made from the poppy?......................... 759

Where is the banyan tree found? Describe its growth.......... 731

To what size does the baobab tree grow? Describe its flower and fruit. To what use is it put by the natives?........ 731

Where do pearls come from? What is mother-of-pearl?....760, 753

For what is the diamond remarkable? What is the value of the ruby?... 760

What is meant by saying that a diamond is of the first water?. 760

What color is the sapphire?................................. 760

In what forms does salt exist? What is rock salt? Mention three localities producing large quantities of salt........ 763

How do scientists believe petroleum to have been formed? Where is it found in abundance? Name four petroleum products. 757

Why is gold valuable? In what forms is it found? Describe the process known as placer mining....................747-748

In what forms does silver occur? Mention extensive silver deposits on the American continent...................... 765

Tell something of the lives and the work of the following naturalists: Linnæus, Audubon, Darwin, Gray, Agassiz, Romanes, Burbank, Jordan, Hornaday, Bailey...................394-482

MISCELLANY

When was the great fire in Chicago? Boston? Baltimore?.106, 517

Tell what is known of the runes used by the early nations of northern Europe... 379

What is the Yule clog?   Describe its attendant festivities... 387

What is the meaning of the term "Gordian knot"?............. 360

Outline the legend of the wandering Jew...................... 364

Who first used the arch in building bridges?.................. 778

Name three noted bridges in Great Britain.   Five in the United States...778-780

State the main characteristics of American bridges............. 779

What does St. Patrick's day commemorate?.................... 852

Name the chief old English holidays.   Give the date of Allhalloween.   Of Candlemas.   Of St. Valentine's day........792, 780, 852

Give the dates of the principal holidays observed in the United States...791-792

In what states is arbor day a legal holiday? Labor day? Jefferson Davis's birthday? Lincoln's birthday? Columbus day?...791-792

Give the history of Thanksgiving day in the United States...... 852

What is the origin of the term "money"? "Pin money"? "Red-letter day"? "Days of grace"?....................829-837, 784

Give the history of the United States flag.   How many stars has it? How many stripes? Why?.......................789, 110

When was the name of the British flag changed to Union Jack? Of what is it formed?................................... 852

To whom is the term "Uncle Sam" applied? "John Bull"? "Brother Jonathan"? Give the origin............852, 794, 780

Give the names of some noted historic giants. Of five dwarfs.790, 786

Tell the story of the Kilkenny cats........................... 364

State the number of degrees conferred in Freemasonry........ 789

Give the weight of a carat. Who owns the largest cut diamonds in existence?..861, 785

Describe various methods of burial among ancient peoples.... 780

What is the color of mourning in China? In Turkey? Egypt? Europe?.. 796

Where is the hall of fame? State its object. How often are new names added?....................................790-791

What is the origin of the word "news"?...................... 831

Explain the origin and the meaning of "Hobson's choice"...... 791

Where did the term "dark horse" originate?.................. 784

Give the location and the height of the following: Eiffel tower, Woolworth building, Washington monument, pyramid of Cheops.. 783

State the origin of the dollar mark........................... 785

Give the origin of the pawnbroker's sign..................... 849

What is camouflage? What are camoufleurs?................. 780

Where did the Christmas tree originate? What was its significance before the Christian era?........................... 782

Give the earliest and the latest date on which Easter may occur. How is the date determined?............................. 792

What is the origin of the belief in the Easter rabbit?........... 792

How many states have adopted the goldenrod as the state flower? What is the flower of your state?................. 852

Give the popular name of each of the following states: New York, Maine, California, Georgia, Michigan, Texas...... 850-851

The people of what state are called Rovers? Creoles? Tar heels? Wolverines? Badgers?....................... 850-851

Give the popular name of your state. Of its people......... 850-851

Where is the Blarney stone? What is the popular superstition in regard to it?.. 777

How many persons out of 100,000 reach the age of 100 years? What percentage of the population dies before the age of seven?.. 795

To what extent has Esperanto been adopted? State its principle. What so-called universal language was invented in 1879? 788-789, 386

What is the legal weight in your state of a bushel of apples? Of wheat? Of onions? Of cotton seed? Of coal?......... 862

Where did the duel originate? Tell something of the practice. 785-786

What part of the country is popularly known as Dixie?........ 785

Give the origin and the meaning of "catching a Tartar"........ 781

Name some trades classed as dangerous by the British parliament. Why?...783-784

How large is the dome of the capitol at Washington? Where is the largest dome in the world?........................ 785

In what respects do gypsies differ from the people among whom they live? When did they first appear in Europe?......... 790

Tell something of the Ku-Klux-Klan........................... 794

Give the origin of the Red Cross societies. When and by whom was the American Red Cross society organized?.........849, 404

By whom were the Nobel prizes founded? For what are they awarded and by whom? How many men in the United States have received Nobel prizes?...................... 849

What is a ship's log? How is it used?...........................794

Why is the barber's pole striped?...........................776-777

Why does a person who is unable to write mark the form of a cross
instead of his name?................................... 849

What is the meaning of black Friday? Blue Stocking? Boy-
cott? Bohemian?..................................... 777

Explain the origin and the meaning of the following words:
Altoona, Minnehaha, Canada, Nevada, Philadelphia.......799-834

Name some books suitable for children under six years of age.... 319

What is the origin of Santa Claus? Give the name of the Dutch
Santa Claus..380, 379

State the meaning of "Tom, Dick, and Harry". Of "Popinjay".
....384, 376

Explain the origin of the loving cup.......................... 368

From what great philosopher does Platonic love receive its
name? What is it?................................... 376

Tell the story of Cinderella.................................. 350

What was the cost of the capitol at Washington? Of St. Peter's
cathedral at Rome?..................................578, 572

Where is the green sea? Why is it so called?................. 817

What is the Bayeux tapestry? Where is it?................... 802

Describe the situation of Monte Carlo. For what is it famous?... 545

What incident is connected with the "black hole of Calcutta"? 777

In what sort of tales do the following characters occur: Jack
Horner, Hop-o'-my-Thumb, Old Mother Hubbard, Jack
the Giant-killer, Jack and the Bean-stalk?..............362, 364

What and where are Cleopatra's needles?..................... 809

Give the origin of the following names: Matterhorn, Mont Blanc,
Spuyten Duyvil.....................................828-842

For what are the swords of Damascus famed?................. 660

Name the "Seven Bibles"................................... 381

Give one version of the story of the seven sleepers............. 381

Of what countries is "God Save the King" the national anthem? 360

Name the seven wonders of the world........................ 849

How many pounds equal a cubic foot of anthracite coal? Of
bituminous coal?.................................... 860

How many cubic inches in a bushel *stricken* measure? *Heap*
measure? What products are measured by heap measure?.. 860

What is the difference in feet between a statute mile and a nau-
tical mile?... 861

When was the parcel post established in the United States? What
do the postal zones represent? Give the limits in size and
weight for mailable parcels. State fee for insurance........ 848

How many cords in a pile of wood 28 ft. long, 6 ft. wide, 7 ft. high?... 860

What is percentage?.. 853

This year's income is $900, which is 12½% more than last year's income.   What was last year's income?................... 853

What is simple interest?   Compound interest?   Exact interest? 853

Find the interest on $600 for 3 years, 4 months, 10 days, at 4%. What is the amount?................................... 853

What is the exact interest on $360 for 90 days at 5%?......... 854

What is commercial discount?   Bank discount?   True discount? 854

A note for $500 payable in 2 months is discounted by a bank. What is the bank discount and what are the proceeds, money being worth 5%?.............................. 855

A man bought a lot for $2,560 and sold it at a gain of 20%. How much did he gain?   What was the selling price?........... 855

What will be the annual income from investing $3,427.50 in 5% stock, purchased at 57, allowing ⅛% brokerage?....... 857

What must I pay for 5% stock that my investment may yield 6%?... 857

A merchant insured his house for $1,500 at ½% annual premium. Find the premium.................................... 856

Find the cost of digging the cellar of a house whose length is 41 ft. 3 in., width 33 ft., depth 8 ft., the cost of excavating being 50 cents a load.................................. 859

Find cost of plastering a room 16 ft. long, 14¾ ft. wide, and 10 ft. high above baseboard, at 45 cents a sq. yd.   The room has two windows, each 7 ft. by 3 ft., and two doors, each 8 ft. by 4½ ft....................................... 858

How many strips of carpeting 1 yd. wide will be required for a room 18 ft. long by 15 ft. wide if the strips are laid lengthwise?   How many yards in each strip?   How many yards will be required for the room?   What will be the cost at $1.25 a yard?.. 858

How many cubic feet of masonry in the walls of a cellar 30 ft. long, 20 ft. wide, outside measurement, the walls to be 9 ft. high and 18 in. thick, deducting 250 cubic feet for openings?.. 859

How many bushels of grain will a bin hold that is 6 ft. long, 3½ ft. wide and 7 ft. high?............................... 860

How many gallons of water will a cistern hold that is 5 ft. in diameter and 8 ft. deep?............................... 860

How many feet of lumber will a log 18 in. in diameter at the smaller end and 14 ft. long yield?........................ 860

INDEX

Africa:
  Egypt, History,............11–12
  Egypt, Literature,..........81–85
  Geography,..............129–130
  Government,.... 131–134
America:
  Geography,.............116–122
  Government,............131–138
  History,.................33–50
  Literature,.............109–114
American History,...........33–50
  Canada,.................46–48
  Colonization,............34–37
  Mexico,.................48–49
  Revolution,..............37–39
  South America,...........49–50
  Union,.................39–45
American Literature,........109–114
Ancient History,.............11–22
  Assyria,....................13
  Babylon,....................13
  Chaldea,...................13
  China,..................12–13
  Egypt,.................11–12
  Greece,.................15–18
  Hebrews,...............13–14
  Japan,.................12–13
  Persia,.................14–15
  Phenicia,...............14–15
  Rome,..................18–22
Arts, Fine,................143–146
Asia:
  Geography,.............127–129
  Government,............131–134
  History,..........12–15, 65–68
  Literature,..............81–85
Asiatic Countries, History,.....65–68
  China,......................68
  Japan,..................66–67
  Saracens,...............65–66
Assyria:
  History,....................13
  Literature,...............81–85
Austria-Hungary:
  Government,............131–134
  History,.....................59
Babylon:
  History,....................13
  Literature,...............81–85
Belgium:
  Government,............131–134
  History,.................63–64
Canada:
  Geography,.............116–121
  Government,............131–134
  History,.................46–48
Capitals, Use of,............70–71

Chaldea:
  History,......................13
  Literature,................81–85
China:
  Government,............131–134
  History,..............12–13, 68
Civics,....................135–138
Commerce,................139–142
Continental Europe, History,...51–64
Denmark:
  Government,............131–134
  History,.....................60
  Literature,...............90–93
Education,................143–146
Egypt:
  History,.................11–12
  Literature,.............. ..81–85
England:
  Canada,..........46–48, 116–121
  Geography,.............122–127
  Government,............131–134
  History,................23–32
  Literature,.............102–109
English, Higher,............77–80
English History,............23–32
  Anglo-Saxon Kings,..........24
  Danish Kings,..............24
  Hanover, House of,........30–32
  Lancaster, House of,.........27
  Norman Kings,..............25
  Plantagenets,............25–26
  Roman Period,..............23
  Saxe-Coburg, House of,.......32
  Saxon Kings,...............25
  Saxons, Coming of the,.......24
  Stuart, House of,.........28–30
  Tudor, House of,.........27–28
  York, House of,.............27
English Literature,.........102–109
Europe:
  Geography,.............122–127
  Government,............131–134
  History,...........15–32, 51–64
  Literature,.............85–109
Europe, Continental, History,..51–64
  Austria-Hungary,.............59
  Belgium,.................63–64
  Denmark,....................60
  France,.................54–57
  Germany,................57–59
  Greece,.....................64
  Holland,.................63–64
  Italy,...................51–52
  Norway,.................60–61
  Portugal,...............53–54
  Russia,.................62–63
  Spain,.................53–54

Europe, Continental, History—Cont'd
  Sweden,....................60–61
  Turkey,...................52–53
France:
  Government,............131–134
  History,...................54–57
  Literature,................95–97
Geography,................115–130
  Africa,..................129–130
  America, North,.........116–121
  America, South,.........121–122
  Asia,....................127–129
  Europe,.................122–127
Germany:
  Government,............131–134
  History,...................57–59
  Literature,................93–95
Government,...............131–138
Greece:
  Government,............131–134
  History,................15–18, 64
  Literature,................85–88
Hebrews, The:
  History,...................13–14
  Literature,................81–85
History,....................11–68
  American,.................33–50
  Ancient,..................11–22
  Asiatic Countries,........65–68
  Continental Europe,......51–64
  English,..................23–32
History, Natural,..........147–150
Holland:
  Government,............131–134
  History,...................63–64
Industry,.................139–142
Invention,................139–142
Italy:
  Government,............131–134
  History,...................51–52
  Literature,................97–99
Japan:
  Government,............131–134
  History,............12–13, 66–67
  Literature,...................102
Language,..................69–80
  Capitals,..................70–71
  Higher English,...........77–80
  Letter Writing,...........75–77
  Punctuation,..............70–71
  Words, Correct Use of,.....71–75
Letter Writing,............75–77
Literature,................81–114
  American,...............109–114
  English,................102–109
  French,...................95–97
  German,..................93–95
  Greek,...................85–88
  Italian,..................97–99
  Japanese,..................102

Literature—Continued
  Latin,....................88–90
  Oriental,.................81–85
  Russian,................100–102
  Scandinavian,............90–93
  Spanish,.................99–100
Mexico:
  Geography,.............116–121
  Government,............131–134
  History,...................48–49
Miscellany,...............151–154
Natural History,..........147–150
North America:
  Geography,.............116–121
  Government,............131–138
  History,...................33–49
Norway:
  Government,............131–134
  History,...................60–61
  Literature,................90–93
Oriental Literature,........81–85
Persia:
  History,...................14–15
  Literature,................81–85
Phenicia:
  History,...................14–15
  Literature,................81–85
Portugal:
  Government,............131–134
  History,...................53–54
Punctuation, Use of,........70–71
Roman Literature,..........88–90
Rome, History of,..........18–22
Russia:
  Government,............131–134
  History,...................62–63
  Literature,..............100–102
Saracens, History,.........65–66
Scandinavian Literature,....90–93
Science,..................143–146
South America:
  Geography,.............121–122
  Government,............131–134
  History,...................49–50
Spain:
  Government,............131–134
  History,...................53–54
  Literature,...............99–100
Sweden:
  Government,............131–134
  History,...................60–61
  Literature,................90–93
Turkey:
  Government,............131–134
  History,...................52–53
United States:
  Geography,.............116–121
  Government,............131–138
  History,...................33–45
Words, Correct Use of,......71–75